TRANSFORMING CITIES
REVIVAL IN THE SQUARE

NICK CORBETT

RIBA Enterprises

© Nick Corbett, 2004
Published by RIBA Enterprises Ltd, 15 Bonhill Street, London EC2P 2EA

ISBN 1 85946 160 3

Stock Code: 37721

British Library Cataloguing in Publications Data
A catalogue record for this book is available from the British Library

Publisher: Steven Cross
Project Editor: Anna Walters
Editor: Alasdair Deas
Designed by: Kneath Associates
Printed in the United Kingdom at the University Press, Cambridge

Photographs by Nick Corbett, unless otherwise indicated.

Cover Image: The Duke of York Square off the King's Road in West London, built by Cadogan in 2003. The architects were Paul Davis and Partners and the landscape architects were Elizabeth Banks Associates. This was the first new square to be built in the Royal Borough of Kensington and Chelsea for over a century. The mix of uses include retail, office, and affordable housing to rent. Courtesy of Adam Parker Photography.

SPONSORED BY

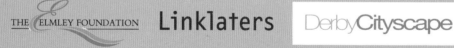

THE ELMLEY FOUNDATION   Linklaters   DerbyCityscape

CONTENTS

Revival in the Square demonstrates the way in which local leaders have devised strategies guiding investment decisions that have significantly transformed urban areas. The great advantage of this approach is that the experience of creating a major new public space gives local authorities the confidence and expertise to improve all of their public spaces. Nick Corbett has direct experience of delivering high quality public space and the book is well illustrated with exciting case studies, many of which have been recently completed. A better quality public realm is a key part of delivering any urban renaissance and I welcome the contribution that this book makes.

Lord Rogers of Riverside, Chief Adviser to the Mayor of London

I welcome *Revival in the Square* because it will give confidence to people who want to challenge the status quo in the design and management of public space. The book demonstrates how a strategic approach can be developed to channel resources in a coherent way to transform the built environment. It shows how uncluttered and joined up public spaces can be built to promote civic values and commercial competitiveness, and how public space can bring people together for a positive, shared experience of urban living.

Jon Rouse, Chief Executive of the Housing Corporation

INTRODUCTION>

REVIVAL IN THE SQUARE

This book provides a new insight into how urban design strategies for new public spaces can transform our cities. It complements the many existing design manuals and publications on urban design theory by showing how ideas can be realised on the ground. It provides a bridge from theory to action. The book is founded upon the premise that the design and management of public space will be a key component of civil renewal. In a recent MORI poll in the UK, 30 per cent of respondents said they did not visit public open spaces because they were afraid of crime.[1] Given such statistics, the themes of this book are of urgent significance, not least for dealing with this sense of fear.

In her book *The Death and Life of Great American Cities*,[2] Jane Jacobs revealed how 20th century planning and architecture were destroying urban quality at great financial and human cost. Jacobs realised how the physical and social components of a successful city fit together, and her book, first published over forty years ago, has served as a foundation for current urban design theory. In the intervening years, many books and studies have been produced that elaborate upon Jacobs' critique and provide practical illustrations of her ideas. Although many studies have been published and public policy has been refined to reflect Jane Jacobs' recommendations, most public space is uninspiring and much of it is perceived to be unsafe. There are many examples of good practice, but the basic mistakes identified by Jacobs remain common practice.

The public realm presents a complex management problem because of the sheer number of legal and professional interests involved. The different governmental, professional, and corporate organisations involved with the design, development, and management of public space have traditionally been divided into separate specialisms, all tackling different parts of the problem. This has resulted in expertise developing in a fragmented way, and in rivalries and communication gaps defining the relationship between the main stakeholders. If the key players involved with the design and management of public space withdraw into their own 'boxes', the gaps between the boxes leave power vacuums. These boxes might be seen as professional cliques of planners or engineers, remote political decision makers, unaccountable advertising companies, or disempowered residents associations.

If the legitimate stakeholders in public space do not effectively communicate and cooperate with each other, the result on the ground is that neglect and antisocial activity begin to drip into the gaps. Most city inhabitants are familiar with the resulting problems of environmental crime, which include fly-posting, graffiti, litter, illegal advertising, begging, soliciting, and drug dealing. A new kind of decision making infrastructure or 'wiring' is required between the stakeholders in public space – this is required to connect, coordinate, and empower the decision makers and other stakeholders. This book shows how the gaps between these groups can be closed through strategic leadership, management, and high-quality design – all to assist in the delivery of an urban renaissance.

The book has two main themes. First, it is about how the decision-making infrastructure can be developed to close the gaps between the key stakeholders involved in the provision of public space, and second, it is about the physical design and management required to create and maintain viable public spaces. The story of the renaissance of Birmingham city centre, in the UK, is a seam that runs through the book and culminates with the detailed case study provided in Chapter Four. The improvements to London's Trafalgar Square are also examined in detail, together with other examples from the USA and Europe.

City squares are used to focus the discussion in this book because they are the most intensively used public spaces – the fact that there has been a recent resurgence in their design also adds to their interest. These squares are public places that derive a unique identity from the buildings, structures, and landscaping that enclose them and give them form. Their identity is also derived from the people that occupy the buildings and spaces and the uses they put them to. The squares that are discussed are of various shapes, sizes, and functions. They often include trees and other landscaping, but crucially they are all an integral part of the built form of the city. They perform an architectural function because they relate to surrounding buildings through their design and use. Creating a city square touches upon many urban design and regeneration issues, and the conclusions reached will often be applicable to other public space and the built environment in general.

The squares used as case studies are public spaces that embrace a mix of land uses, such as residences, businesses, and entertainment uses, and which have a high degree of access from the surrounding city. By concentrating on public squares, there will be a focus on creating dynamic places where there is the capacity for crowds to gather and where seeds can be sown for the development of community.

Urban design is about creating buildings and public spaces that interact with each other and result in visually stimulating, safe, and sustainable settlements. Urban designers seek to understand the three-dimensional qualities that provide people with clear and satisfying images of the city, and which make the city readable and navigable. Through identifying the key physical components that define the city and its public spaces we can begin to understand how to create a more legible city environment and how public space becomes an integral part of this urban morphology.

Many politicians in all levels of government, and from all parts of the political spectrum, appear to be concerned that the quality of life of city residents is being frustrated by antisocial behaviour and environmental crime within public space. There is an increasing political engagement with public space due to perceptions of lawlessness within some areas of the world's most prosperous cities.

In American cities, such as New York, local business and residents groups have taken direct action over the design and management of their public spaces through Business Improvement Districts (BIDs), and these are now beginning to operate in the UK. Through BIDs, community groups have taken control of public spaces where traditional forms of governance had left a power vacuum. This was demonstrated in Bryant Park in New York, which became the haunt of drug dealers until the local community reclaimed the space.

Across the urbanised world, environmental sustainability is high on the political agenda – this has implications for urban design. In most large cities, wherever there is strong political leadership, attempts are now being made to make city centres attractive places to live in, and to increase the density of new development. This serves to regenerate derelict industrial landscapes, to accommodate housing demand, and to prevent further urban encroachment upon the open countryside. If people can be encouraged to live in the city, where there is a high building density and a mix of land uses, they are likely to be physically closer to their work place and to a range of essential services. This closer proximity reduces the need to travel, and so reduces car dependence and the associated traffic, accidents, noise, and air pollution.

It is vital to maintain 'liveability' in a large city. As building density increases so too does the need for public open space – and the need for considerate neighbours. The city square can provide visual relief and recreational open space within a densely developed area, and it can also serve to promote standards in public behaviour. If people are to be aware of the complexity and variety of the society they are a part of, and if they are to appreciate notions of civic identity and respect for others, there must be a place where they can occasionally see and experience a diverse cross section of that society. When people can actively participate in life within the public realm, they learn how to conduct themselves within it. This is especially important for developing ideas about citizenship. By simply standing in a lively public square, where different age groups and different members of society are gathered together, there is a shared experience that evokes a positive sense of participation. In urban areas where there are no well-used public spaces, public life and civility become seriously eroded. There is a retreat to the privacy and potential isolation of home, where media empires can sift the information we receive through the television, newspapers, internet, and radio.

If the design, implementation, and management of new city squares is undertaken through a partnership approach that engages with local people, urban character and social cohesion can be strengthened. City squares can then contribute to a richer mix of facilities that attract both local people and visitors, and can help to make a city more competitive in attracting mobile investment within the global marketplace.

It is helpful to understand why city squares have been developed by different communities through history, and to establish the demands that these spaces have been expected to satisfy. Historical analysis can help to establish themes that squares have been developed to address through the ages, such as the need to provide a population with a place for festivals or with a symbolic focal point that reinforces their collective identity. An understanding of the past can often inform the present and indicate how the future might unfold, and so this book makes some reference to historical urban development.

Political leaders, and those who seek power, have sought to control activities within key public spaces and have created new city squares and processional routes to symbolise their power and control. For example, in the first half of the 20th century, Mussolini used urban design to symbolise a link between himself and Rome's glorious past. He attempted to do this by demolishing the medieval district that had grown over the ancient Roman Forum and creating a new processional route over it. This route linked the ancient Coliseum with the city square of Piazza Venezia, where Mussolini resided in the Vittoriano Palace.

To an undemocratic administration, a city square is a threatening cradle for unconformist gatherings and demonstrations. Tiananmen Square in Beijing, China, is known around the world because of the killings of antigovernment protestors there in 1990. In Franco's Spain, strict controls, which lasted for decades, were placed over the use of public squares. The resurgence in the design of new Spanish squares, especially as seen in Barcelona, celebrates a new civic confidence. Effective management regimes now need to be developed to maintain the investment made in these new spaces.

Today, a healthy democracy is expected to be interested in encouraging public participation in urban design. Across the world, there has been particular interest among politicians and professionals involved with the built environment to make the great industrial cities more liveable. Urban design, and in particular the creation of new public space, is now often seen as an essential part of an urban regeneration programme. The importance of the task is demonstrated by the unprecedented global urbanisation that occurred in the second half of the 20th century. The result of this has been that, for the first time in world history, most people live in urban areas. The impact of large cities upon humanity has grown massively. In 1900 there were 13 cities in the world with populations exceeding one million – there are currently 284. At least 24 cities now have populations exceeding 10 million, and several metropolitan areas' populations exceed 20 million.

Above. Citizens from different communities in Beiruit, Lebanon, gather in Nejmeh Square. This is the city's main public space, beautifully restored after years of civil war. (Courtesy of Solidere.)

The economic, cultural and technological developments in large cities have led to large-scale inward migration and urban sprawl. The people and markets in these vast urban areas are interconnected as never before, especially due to advances in information technology. The spread and mixing of peoples has resulted in cities with people from a variety of ethnic backgrounds, ideologies, faiths, and income groups. The results have led to diversity and opportunity – but also to tension and fear. A degree of acceptance between people has been necessary for peaceful coexistence in many culturally diverse urban areas. Perhaps a notion that we have more in common than separating us has supported this. It is often people's identification with a city itself that helps to serve as a bridge between cultural differences. This can be seen in Beirut in Lebanon, where reconstruction works are providing new public places that are bringing together people who were previously separated by civil war.

Some people have dealt with the challenges of urban life by retreating as far as possible into the private realm – living in gated developments, shopping in malls, and relaxing and keeping fit in private clubs. The principal criterion for entrance into these private spaces is usually the ability to pay. If the wealthier members of society continue to retreat into private space, the public realm will suffer from a lack of investment and could increasingly be seen as a place for the 'have-nots'. To prevent this from happening, and to maximise choice for all sections of the community, the design and management of the public realm needs to compete with the quality of the private realm.

The developed world now exists in an information age – a time when the communication and delivery of ideas is rapidly expanding the frontiers of our knowledge and experience. Powerful interests present us with their ideas and suggestions through a multitude of media, seeking to influence us and to shape the world we live in. At one level, the increasing flow of information has rapidly changed many aspects of our lives – it influences cultural and political priorities, even where and how we live. The information age has influenced the way that we interact with cities, and the way that we shape them. This book examines how we can design and manage public space in a way that responds to these changing expectations. Through effective urban design, the social and economic forces operating upon cities can be channelled to create attractive, safe, dynamic, and socially inclusive public places. Such places reinforce a collective identity and sense of belonging throughout a diverse urban population. The design of public space is especially important in bringing people together and in creating a shared experience of a city. The main square is often closely associated with the unique identity of a particular city.

For as long as cities have existed, the city square has been a focus for the public life of the urban population. While many city squares were neglected during the 20th century, often being dominated by traffic and car parking, cities and their regions are now competing in a global marketplace and so the image of individual cities is increasingly important. Governments around the developed world are encouraging city authorities to work with the private sector to invest in urban design and regeneration, and new city squares are providing a focus for this activity.

Given the world's growing urban population and the need to make cities 'liveable' for their inhabitants, issues related to city design are becoming a greater political priority. The themes of this book will therefore be of particular interest to those who make decisions on the way that cities are developed, and to those who seek to influence and advise decision makers.

While urban design principles are often cited as objectives in new development initiatives, the performance of the resulting public space often falls disappointingly short of expectations. Realising urban design objectives is difficult in practice due to the complexity of the development process. For example, a development project will typically involve finding the right location, assembling land, organising finance, ordering the priorities of strategic planning, site planning, and architectural design, and maintaining momentum and political support.

Professional institutions have recently found common ground in the cause for urban design and regeneration. In December 1997 the Urban Design Alliance (UDAL) was formed in the UK by the professional organisations and groups with an interest in urban design and regeneration. This alliance has grown and has already helped to break through the guarded barriers between the different professions. This kind of cooperation helps to unite fragmented sources of expertise and information – it closes the gaps and informs the national debate on urban issues.

For urban designers to be effective they need to be able to influence the process through which the built environment is developed. This requires an understanding of a broad range of disciplines, including politics, planning, architecture, finance, law, and project management. These issues are addressed in Chapter One of this book, which focuses on the role of urban design strategies in managing the development process. Whatever the professional backgrounds of urban designers, they will need to understand an area's physical structure before creating new public spaces for it. Chapters Two and Three of this book therefore focus upon the physical structure of the city to help ensure that new squares and public spaces can relate well to the surrounding urban context. Issues relating to location, movement, access, legibility, form, scale, and use are all discussed. Chapter Four provides a detailed case study of Birmingham's urban renaissance.

SUMMARY OF THE CHAPTERS

Chapter One: *Making place from space* examines the processes of developing high-quality public space, especially through the use of urban design strategies and partnerships of key stakeholders. The chapter shows how the development process can be managed to accommodate the requirements of investors, developers, financiers, landowners, politicians, planners, and the collective demands of the urban community. Urban design strategies are shown to be vision documents that can be used to bring together stakeholders under a shared banner, and thereby close the gaps between them.

The chapter investigates how the management of space within squares, and within the buildings around public space, can promote urban vitality. For example, through programmes of special events designed to encourage use, participation, and social inclusion. It addresses issues of management and maintenance, and suggests criteria for monitoring the long-term success of new public spaces.

Publications that focus on the processes of creating and managing responsive public spaces, and therefore relate to Chapter One, include:

■ *People Places,* by Clare Cooper Marcus and Carolyn Francis[3]
■ *The Social Life of Small Urban Spaces,* by William H. Whyte[4]
■ *Urban Design: Street and Square*, by Cliff Moughtin[5]
■ *The City Assembled*, by Spiro Kostof[6]
■ *Public Spaces, Public Life*, by Jan Gehl and Lars Gemzoe[7]
■ *Public Places – Urban Spaces,* by Matthew Carmona, Tim Heath, Tanner Oc and Steven Tiesdell.[8]

These publications also examine the influence of public space on the cultural life and values of urban society. They show how well-used public spaces can strengthen the collective consciousness of the urban population. This new book adds to the debate by showing how high-quality, joined-up spaces that promote the image and competitiveness of a city can actually be built.

Chapter Two: *Location and movement* focuses upon the prerequisite design feature for a city square: the right location. The chapter demonstrates how choosing the right site depends on access, movement patterns, legibility, and servicing arrangements. It examines how the site for a city square needs to be where people can easily access it, and how it should be located where people are headed to, or are passing through, in relatively large numbers. Kevin Lynch's book *The Image of the City* interprets the city as a series of paths, nodes, landmarks, views, edges, and districts. This language is helpful in understanding how a city square and connecting streets fit into the surrounding urban area, and his terminology informs the discussion (see Appendix I for an adapted typology of these urban components).

The chapter shows how establishing a city square may require urban restructuring to create an accessible site, and how a new square can serve as a model for design proposals within a broader strategy for renewing an urban area. The way in which movement patterns influence the city square and the image of the city are explored by examining how Trafalgar Square in London has been transformed through the 'World Squares' initiative. This completed project is challenging many of London's boroughs to rethink the way that people can interrelate with existing public spaces.

Chapter Three: *Physical form and robustness* begins with a brief discussion of how city squares and processional routes have become enduring features in the layout of cities. A historical analysis shows that, as well as providing spatial relief and a place for the expression of cultural values, city squares have been used for spectacles and major events that have shaped history. Classic books that cover the historical development of squares and streets around the world include:

■ *The City in History*, by Lewis Mumford[9]
■ *Town and Square*, by Paul Zucker[10]
■ *The History of Urban Form Before the Industrial Revolution*, by A. E. J. Morris.[11]

These books, and others, identify the human needs that public spaces have been designed and managed to satisfy since ancient times. They help to inform this book's discussion of the potential role of public space in influencing the life of a city and even a nation.

The chapter goes on to examine how the various parts of a square cay be physically arranged to form a coherent architectural composition. It establishes principles to assist in designing a square that can have practical use, visual cohesion, physical comfort, and visual delight. It covers practical issues, such as designing the transition from a street to a square and the relationship between size, shape, and sense of enclosure.

The chapter focuses on the physical form and robustness of public space. Physical form and robustness are closely interrelated, together they determine how visually coherent a space is and how useful it is to the urban community. The discussion on robustness investigates the significance of layout, massing, and landscaping for the microclimate and use of space. It explores how different components of space, such as seating and public art, can be arranged to generate activity, and how mixed-use developments can bring together residential communities, employment, and public facilities (such as modern public libraries and multimedia centres).

Existing publications that serve as practical design manuals and which complement the discussion on design principles in Chapters Two and Three include:

- *Responsive Environments*, by Ian Bentley, Alan Alcock, Paul Murrain, Sue McGlynn and Graham Smith[12]
- *The Image of the City*, by Kevin Lynch[13]
- *Paving the Way*, by Alan Baxter Associates for CABE[14]
- *The Urban Design Compendium*, by Llewelyn-Davies for English Partnerships and the Housing Corporation[15]
- *The Art of Building Cities*, by Camillo Sitte.[16]

Chapter Four: *Renaissance in Birmingham* provides a case study that demonstrates how some of the themes of this book have been delivered on the ground. The chapter shows how an urban design strategy has been used in Birmingham in the UK to develop city squares and connecting streets to regenerate the city centre. Birmingham's transformation demonstrates the importance of high-quality public space, especially in the form of interconnected public squares and streets, in the delivery of effective urban renewal. The case study shows how an urban design strategy can be used to market a city and to increase its standing within the international marketplace. The problems encountered in the delivery of the regeneration are also discussed, especially in relation to creating mixed-use urban developments.

In conclusion, this book has been produced to show how public spaces can be designed, developed, and managed to strengthen the identity of urban areas and to deliver an urban renaissance.

CHAPTER ONE>

CHAPTER ONE
MAKING PLACE FROM SPACE

Producing an urban design strategy can assist in creating a vision, which is essential for implementing complex development projects. These strategies, which are sometimes referred to as urban design frameworks, need to be more focused than traditional policy documents or master plans. They need to provide for coordinated action by a partnership to secure implementation of commonly agreed objectives. The objectives of an urban design strategy need to be based on the aspirations of its partners – these partners will be stakeholders from community, private, and public interests. The objectives also need to be based on the constraints and opportunities posed by the study area and by financial realities. An urban design strategy might include the following components, and these help to structure the rest of the chapter:

■ A *vision statement*, signed by all partners, together with a plan showing the boundaries of the study area and a set of objectives against which the success of the project can be judged.
■ A *programme* that explains how the leadership and organisational structure of the partnership has been created to develop and deliver the strategy, outlining who is responsible for what. This should also include a *methodology* of the working practices and processes to be followed in delivering the project to an agreed timetable.

- A *contextual analysis* that describes the character of the area and its people and explains the background to the project. This should also illustrate and justify the physical boundaries chosen for the study area.
- An *implementation strategy* that addresses funding by identifying where resources are coming from and how they will be allocated, and provides a *phasing strategy* with a timetable for delivery of the whole process.
- A *community participation strategy* showing how the local community and other key stakeholders are to be involved in developing, approving, and implementing the strategy and the proposals within it.
- A *management plan* to show how the vitality and commercial competitiveness of new public places will be maintained over time.

Producing an urban design strategy through a partnership approach can provide a clearer understanding of an area and how it works. Producing a contextual analysis is essential for achieving this – it provides the physical and social information that will inform decision making. By analysing how the various components of the built environment fit together within the study area, the contextual analysis will also provide a kind of health check for the built environment, showing how its performance could be improved. Both the physical and human geography aspects of the contextual analysis will be explored in this and subsequent chapters.

The ultimate goal of the urban design strategy is to serve as the vehicle that brings together people and resources to develop an area under the banner of an agreed vision.

CREATING PARTNERSHIPS

Producing an urban design strategy and developing new buildings and public spaces clearly requires considerable organisational, financial, and professional resources. Different organisations and individuals can contribute different abilities, expertise, and resources. These need to be brought together to form an effective partnership that can produce and implement an urban design strategy and proposals for new city squares.

The public sector

It is often the role of a city council to facilitate the partnership, bring together the different players, and provide the impetus for the vision. The local authority is a partner that is geographically fixed to the study area and should therefore have a strong long-term commitment to it. The local authority is also democratically accountable to local citizens. If an urban design strategy is backed by a strong champion from the local authority, ideally an executive mayor with a reasonably long term of office, this can add to market confidence and to the certainty that the vision will be implemented. The public sector can also sometimes provide land, finance, and possibly in-house professional expertise. Furthermore, when an urban design strategy focuses upon land that is derelict or without a registered owner, or when there is a complex pattern of ownership, public-sector planning powers are necessary to assemble the different parcels of land in preparation for redevelopment.

An urban design strategy will benefit from having the committed support of influential local politicians and officers of the local authority, who will have access to crucial resources. They can also provide advice in satisfying statutory procedures, such as the need to gain planning consents. As with all partners involved in the production and implementation of the strategy, public-sector figures need to be able to inspire confidence in the partnership and strategy by working in a responsive and innovative way, rather than falling back into a simple mode of regulation.

The private sector

The private sector is more experienced in managing the risk involved in financing development and in providing a dynamic and cost-effective approach to development. The survival of private-sector developers is dependent upon their ability to manage risk, and as such they are likely to make a dynamic and realistic contribution towards any partnership.

Private finance is usually required to meet the costs of developing new city squares or other aspects of a regeneration strategy. Offering a share of the development's profits or part ownership of built assets may attract private investment companies to enter into partnership arrangements. When this is the case, legal contracts are required to clarify responsibilities and to determine how future profits and resources will be allocated. It is common practice for public-sector partners to assemble the development sites required for implementing a strategy, and for private developers to take over implementation on the ground from there.

The community sector

Local communities represent pools of knowledge on how areas function for those that live and work there. When local people are respected as experts on their locality, and when they or their representatives are members of a partnership, they are more likely to participate in consultation exercises and to develop a caring sense of ownership of new squares.

In Europe and the USA, the empowering of local communities through the development of urban regeneration partnerships is often cited as a political objective. This inclusive approach benefits the implementation of strategies in a practical way and such interaction is healthy for democracy (see Ref. 17). In reality, people living in run-down areas may find it hard to exercise influence within a partnership made up of experienced professionals and politicians, each arriving with their own agenda and being well versed in the language of planning and development. Before a community can be 'empowered' it needs to have the confidence, skills, knowledge, and language to understand and influence the rules of the game. Community training in basic skills is therefore necessary in some situations. Strategies for engaging with local communities will be discussed in more depth later in this chapter.

Partnerships

Partnerships formed between the public, private, and community sectors have become commonplace since the 1990s, especially in regeneration areas. A partnership between these three different 'expert' groups – public, private, and community – can ensure that urban design objectives are achieved in a realistic way. A partnership approach is also more likely to develop the collective identity of the local community and to be satisfying for those involved in the development process.

It was the public–private partnerships developed in North American cities that inspired British leaders to develop them in the UK in the early 1980s. However, public–private partnerships had already existed in various forms in the UK for over fifty years, having originated in the post-war period. The reconstruction of Britain's blitzed cities was often based on a partnership between local authorities, who provided land, and private developers, who provided capital for development. This was at a time when land markets were weak and commercial developers thin on the ground, a situation reflected in some run-down inner city areas today. In February 1944, the report of the British Government's Advisory Panel on the Reconstruction of City Centres, advising on the rebuilding of blitzed city centres, stated that: 'The development of a site should properly involve a partnership between the ground lessor (the local authority), who provides the capital for land, and the building lessee, who provides the capital for the erection of buildings.'

In February 1946, the Central Advisory Committee on Estate Development and Management provided a vision of how they saw these public–private partnerships developing:[18]

The contract between the Local Authority and developers should be strictly defined and exist as a background to their relationship. But the spirit rather than the letter of the contract between them should govern their dealings with each other. Their relationship should be that of partners in a joint undertaking, it should be personal and it should be human.

Unfortunately, these early agreements tended to benefit the few large developers that existed after the war rather than local communities, especially when local authorities agreed to low long-term ground rents in return for their land. It often took local authorities many years to establish the ground rules that would ensure they received reasonable returns.

In the 1960s, two government guidance bulletins were produced – *Town Centres: Approach to Renewal* (1962)[19] and *Town Centres: Cost and Control of Redevelopment* (1963)[20] – which stated that the best way to accommodate growing car use in city centres was to redevelop them through public–private partnerships. These guidance notes also sought to establish the use of development briefs and competitive tendering to ensure that private developers did not become too dominant within partnerships.

Soon after the publication of these documents, the modernist Bullring shopping centre was developed in Birmingham, which was to serve as a model for other city centre redevelopment schemes across the UK. The Bullring shopping centre blighted part of Birmingham's city centre for several decades, but as we will see in Chapter Four, the Bullring has now been redeveloped through another form of partnership. This time the vision has been supported by an urban design strategy, by a strong elected council leader, and by wider community involvement.

ORGANISATION AND LEADERSHIP
Principal appointments
For an urban design strategy to maintain momentum and credibility, it needs to be underpinned by political leadership – a 'design champion' who can satisfy community expectations and ensure that implementation of urban design objectives occurs in a financially feasible way.

From an early stage, this champion needs to capture the imagination of all involved in the process by working towards a shared vision for change. This vision needs to provide clear goals that different groups can work towards. The vision can then drive the strategy forward and provide the common ground that unites all members of a partnership together. The champion needs to be aware of basic urban design objectives (which are summarised in the *Contextual analysis* section later in this chapter), and of basic good practice. They also need to be sure that all other partners are equally informed.

The key issues for an urban design strategy to address will most likely be discussed when the stakeholders are brought together for a meeting at the start of the process. These early meetings are essential for establishing the outline strategy and for understanding what the resource implications are likely to be. The design champion will ideally serve as the chair of the partnership organisation, and will have to ensure that members of the partnership and of the professional team are respected authorities in their respective disciplines. These lead figures need to be team players who can discern pubic opinion – they should also be able to provide the partnership with a convincing image.

The individuals who sit on a partnership board are, in effect, the governing body, and they are ultimately responsible for the strategy and the proposals within it. Whichever form of partnership structure is used, the chairman needs to be well known and respected, and should be capable of providing leadership. The development of the urban design strategy in Birmingham in the UK, and of the strategy developed by the city of Toronto in Canada for the transformation of Dundas Square (which will be elaborated upon shortly), depended upon well-known city councillors performing a leadership role. In both cases the leaders rallied together key people from the different community and business organisations and successfully dealt with opposition.

When public resources are being invested to implement the proposals in an urban design strategy, the partnership chairman needs to make it clear that this investment is to meet the additional costs of creating a high-quality urban environment, rather than increasing profit margins. All of the private, public, and community partners, together with any other investors and contractors, need to agree to the objectives of the strategy. They need to be involved with the production of the strategy from the beginning to ensure they share the urban design vision. This can help to avoid weakening the vision due to cost cutting. Primary objectives should be commitment to design excellence and to best value, for example by taking into account whole-life costs and the needs of all final users.

Continuity of leadership is important to maintain momentum during the long life of an urban design strategy. When visionary leaders are in for the long haul, they become storehouses of knowledge and experience specific to the project. They build up professional relationships with relevant people and can steer a course through the storms that could otherwise cause the strategy to founder. In Birmingham it was the production of the City Centre Design Strategy, published with the backing of a strong council leader in 1990, that has enabled coordinated investment for over a decade in a way that has transformed the city. Strong leadership is required to ensure that everyone involved in the development process is aware of the vision and of the objectives within the urban design strategy. This includes all of the partnership stakeholders, the professional team, consultants and contractors, local officials, and those who will manage and occupy the completed scheme.

To ensure that everyone is maintaining the vision and that design standards remain high, project management mechanisms that allow for regular reviews of how the process is proceeding need to be in place. Vital feedback from these reviews needs to be given to the partnership to keep them informed and up-to-date. While the chairman performs a leadership role, a project director is also usually necessary for organising the production and implementation of an urban design strategy. Both the chairman and the project director need to present a unified front to ensure that both the local community and investors in the outside world are filled with confidence. The chairman and the project director need to be constantly engaged in binding the partners together to form an effective team, and both should also be able to speak with authority on behalf of the partnership. They need to provide an effective, streamlined management structure so that executive decisions can be made quickly and in an informed way. This helps to provide the kind of confidence and certainty that can attract financial investors into an urban area.

A project director is usually either a paid consultant or a direct employee of the partnership, or they may be seconded from one of the partner organisations. If a project manager is not appointed there is likely to be a lack of coordination, communication, accountability, and responsibility, and the effectiveness of the partnership will therefore suffer. The partnership's leaders have a formidable and dynamic task. As we will see in Chapter Four, it can take more than ten years to implement an urban design strategy, and over this time key personnel may come and go. When these changes occur, a strong champion needs to be in place to take the helm and keep the vision on course.

At the very start of the process when key stakeholders meet to discuss issues and objectives, the project director needs to be focused upon producing an outline strategy. They need to identify the people who are going to be involved, what their responsibilities are likely to be, what kind of resources are going to be required, and what lines of communication and reporting mechanisms will be necessary.

It is likely there will be many different projects being delivered at different times under the umbrella of an urban design strategy. These different projects will require their own delivery mechanisms and procurement, but the leaders behind the urban design strategy need to influence the design and development of all projects to ensure they fit within the overall vision. The project director for the urban design strategy may be in the best position to act as a single point of contact for managing the design process and for ensuring the partnership retains overall control of all major developments within the study area.

Professional advisers

A partnership that has embarked upon delivering an urban design strategy will need to rely not only on a project director, but also on other skilled professional advisers. There will usually need to be professional input from

- urban designers
- town planners
- landscape architects
- financiers
- builders
- architects
- surveyors
- lawyers
- artists
- estate agents.

Professional services are required to
- manage the project
- help formulate the vision
- organise public consultation
- produce the contextual analysis
- manage the production of the strategy
- produce designs
- promote the vision and market investment opportunities
- produce financial appraisals
- raise finances
- construct buildings and landscaping
- manage and maintain the development once it is complete.

The professionals serving a partnership are often from private-sector consultants employed by one of the partner organisations, or by the whole partnership if it is a legal entity – as was the case in the redevelopment of the city centre of Manchester in the UK following large-scale destruction caused by a terrorist bomb.

The professional team will need to include qualified architects, with practices and individuals being carefully selected based on experience and the specific demands of the project. A competitive process can be helpful in comparing the attributes of different architectural practices. However, care is required to ensure that there is community involvement in the production of the brief for any architectural competition.

Given the importance of selecting the right team, the partnership will probably need to take expert advice in the selection of consultants. Alternatively, professional staff could be from an in-house team from a local authority or other partner organisation. More probably, professional advisers will be from a mixture of both the public and private sectors.

Whatever the case, it is essential that the professional advisers perform as a team. They will need to meet regularly together, and some form of team-building exercises can help to quickly integrate them with each other and with the members of the partnership. Some kind of 'celebration' to mark key stages of the process can assist with this. Taking this extra level of care can have dramatic results in terms of maintaining trust and motivation.

The inclusion of property and real estate expertise within the professional team will also be essential. When a strategy includes the development of new public spaces and buildings, this specialist advice will be required to research the local property market, ensure that proposals can be realistically implemented, and establish the commercial viability of different uses. These professional advisers will realise that some assumptions about the value of land are market-sensitive and that making them public could affect the values they need to protect. Property experts will assist in producing a financially viable phasing plan for implementation of the strategy. Surveyors will also be required to establish other development costs, such as building materials and labour.

Partnership structures

A real partnership approach between the public, private, and community stakeholders requires some kind of legally defined decision-making organisation which is financially accountable and capable of entering into development contracts. Government money can usually only be awarded to organisations with a legal entity capable of meeting the liabilities that flow from their conditions of granting funds.

A 'joint venture company' can be an effective way of bringing different partners together in a single partnership organisation. This company can then produce an urban design strategy to regenerate an area, produce a funding strategy, bid for public funding, enter into contracts to access private finance, and let contracts to develop new buildings, public spaces, and other infrastructure.

A joint venture company was the vehicle used to implement the urban design strategy and master plan that was produced for the redevelopment of central Manchester after the terrorist attack. This company, Manchester Millennium Ltd, used a partnership approach to secure major new development for the city within a very limited time scale. A showpiece of the redevelopment is Exchange Place, a new city square created from a run-down area that previously had a main road cutting through it. This new square has been developed as a focal point for the rebuilding of the city.

Joint venture companies are focused and goal-orientated because the partners have a legal duty to work in the best interests of the company. However, this can create a conflict of interests, especially for community representatives, whose allegiance has to be given first to the interests of the company rather than to the interests of the people they represent. In effect, the members of the partnership are no longer representatives but delegates.

A simpler alternative to forming a joint venture company is to form an independent partnership committee, which can be used to oversee the production of an urban design strategy, funding strategy, and implementation of projects. As with any partnership, this committee needs to be representative of the private, public, and community stakeholders.

The relatively informal status of a partnership committee means it is dependent on a partner organisation providing staff and offices with established procedures for accounting for public finance and other regulatory requirements. This partner usually acts as the legally defined 'accountable body'. Given their local accountability, local authorities often take on this role. With this management structure, care is required to ensure that all partners remain fully involved in decision making on an equal basis, and that the local authority has the resources to handle the extra responsibility. It is helpful if the chairman of the partnership committee is also the head of the accountable body, to ensure that decisions made by the partnership are implemented with high priority.

CONTEXTUAL ANALYSIS

A contextual analysis identifies what the existing character of an area is, and begins to indicate how it could be transformed. Everywhere is somewhere, and the analysis within a contextual analysis helps to establish the elements of local distinctiveness that can be strengthened through new development. To do this, the regional characteristics, as well as more local factors, need to be identified, in terms of both physical and human geography. This book aims to show how urban character and identity can be promoted through the development of public space, and, as such, most of the discussion should help to inform the production of a contextual analysis.

The process of producing the contextual analysis can begin with a SWOT analysis to identify the factors (strengths, weaknesses, opportunities, and threats) that could affect the development of a responsive public realm. A key consideration to be addressed by the contextual analysis is movement – for example, identification of how routes can be developed to knit new public spaces into the surrounding area. Given the importance of movement and location in the development of city squares, these issues are covered in detail in Chapter Two, with case studies from London and Copenhagen.

The UK Government's advisory Commission for Architecture and the Built Environment (CABE), in its document *By Design*,[21] suggests that the physical character of an area is made up of the following design aspects, which provide useful headings for the contextual analysis.

- Urban structure: the framework of routes and spaces.
- Urban grain: the pattern of blocks, plots, and buildings.
- Landscape: shape, form, ecology, and natural features.
- Density and mix: the amount of development and the range of uses.
- Scale: height and massing.
- Appearance: details and materials.

Throughout the production of the contextual analysis it is helpful to be mindful of the objectives of urban design. CABE suggests the following generic objectives.[22]

- Character: a place with its own identity.
- Continuity and enclosure: a place where public and private spaces are clearly distinguished.
- Quality of the public realm: a place with attractive and successful outdoor areas (i.e. areas which are valued by people who use them or pass through them).
- Ease of movement: a place that is easy to get to and move through.
- Legibility: a place that has a clear image and is easy to understand.
- Adaptability: a place that can change easily.
- Diversity: a place with variety and choice.

The contextual analysis can begin to show how city squares can be developed to model all of these objectives, especially because they contain intensive interactions between people, buildings, and spaces. Urban designers and decision makers need to maintain the 'big picture', always considering how lessons learned on model projects can be applied across a wider urban region. It may be helpful for the conclusions in the contextual analysis to make some reference to how the study area fits into this bigger picture. In areas where the existing character is viewed by local people as being negative or harmful, the wider region can be explored to identify positive models for re-imaging.

Other issues that need to be addressed in the contextual analysis relate to natural features, such as topography and geology, and to engineering issues, such as provision of services and remediation of contaminated land. Social and economic issues to be addressed include the priorities and policies of national, regional, and local government. The contextual analysis will need to be a 'live' document, evolving as new pieces of information come to light – for example, after engaging with the local community or following ground-exploration works.

User groups

Analysis of local population characteristics can be a key part of the contextual analysis to ensure that provision of public space is in response to local needs. The section later in this chapter under the heading *Community participation strategies* shows how the priorities of the local community can be established.

The ancient Roman architect Vitruvius Pollio was concerned about the visual qualities of the public square, and also about its robustness for practical use. He realised that it was essential to understand the user requirements of the space before the space could be properly designed, and that if the space did not accurately reflect the function it was to serve, the design would not be successful. He stated that the space within the square should not be so large that it would be difficult to fill – any events held within the square would then appear unsuccessful. As with any event, if the venue is only half full, the atmosphere suffers. The contextual analysis therefore needs to understand the requirements of the people who will be using the proposed new public spaces. If the city square is to be designed as a robust space, along the lines suggested by Vitruvius, a prerequisite in the design process will be to analyse who the potential users of the space are likely to be. Establishing the potential catchment area of a square can help identify its users.

A study of eight public spaces in San Francisco in the USA found that most people had walked an average distance of 275 m to get there.[22] Cooper Marcus and Francis[3] state that the authors of a study in Sydney in Australia reached a similar conclusion. San Francisco is a relatively high-density city and resembles the layout and form of many European cities. The findings of the Lieberman study are therefore loosely transferable to many similar urban contexts. However, there will be many considerations that affect the catchment area of a new square, including the effectiveness of local public transport, the location of any transit stops or public transport interchanges, the location of physical barriers (such as busy roads or a railway line), and the location of other competing public open spaces.

If the Lieberman study is used as a guide, a circle with a radius of approximately 275 m drawn around the potential site for a square will generally represent the catchment area, i.e. the area within convenient walking distance. Within this catchment area, the socio-economic details of the population need to be considered. Relevant data should cover both the resident and working populations, and include their age, sex, ethnicity, and employment. This kind of demographic information should be included in the contextual analysis part of the urban design strategy. It will help to build a picture of the kind of services and activities that the square should provide.

Connections with the past

If the contextual analysis investigates the historical background of an area, it can inform the design process by adding meaning and value to a location. This kind of research can be undertaken through talks with local historians, long-term residents,

Left. Blue plaques in London provide interesting facts about the connections between buildings and people.

and by studying legal records and archives covering occupancy, ownership, and use of buildings and land. The historical analysis can assist in producing a name for a new city square or for the buildings around it, or it could result in a historical theme being adopted for public art within a square.

Another way that historical information can be used to promote the identity of a city square is to erect plaques on buildings associated with famous people or important local events. People are usually fascinated with facts about the history of their area and so the contextual analysis should give them as much relevant information as possible.

FUNDING AND IMPLEMENTATION

One of the main reasons for creating partnerships is to bring together the resources required for regeneration. A number of innovative ways have been developed to gather these resources and to use them to best effect.

Acquisition and control of strategic sites

Birmingham City Council has spent over ten years implementing its urban design strategy by using a variety of funding approaches and partnerships. At the start of the process the council determined that new and improved city squares and interconnected streets were to be developed. To achieve this the council acted as a land speculator, buying key sites that would be required to implement the urban design strategy. The council purchased these sites when the market was relatively depressed, and when the market was more buoyant they were sold, with legally binding development agreements, to private developers. These agreements required the purchaser to implement the objectives of the urban design strategy so far as they reasonably related to their site.

Strategic sites with uncooperative owners were compulsory purchased. This is how the council secured the development of Brindley Place, which has become a focal point for the city's urban renaissance. In developing other new squares Birmingham City Council implemented the objectives of the urban design strategy through raising finance itself, and through applying for government and European Union grants. Birmingham's urban design strategy and the vision of its leaders have kept these projects, which are programmed to continue for another ten years, rolling forward. The transformation of Birmingham city centre is discussed in more detail in Chapter Four.

A form of partnership was used to develop Dundas Square, a major new public space at the heart of Toronto in Canada, to help promote a new world image for the city. Developing this square involved collaboration between the city authorities,

Above. Brindley Place, Birmingham, which resulted from a strategy that helped to focus the city council's development control powers, and led to the council acting as a land speculator.

Below. Sketch of Dundas Square in Toronto, Canada – a flagship project that forms part of a broader regeneration strategy. (City of Toronto.)

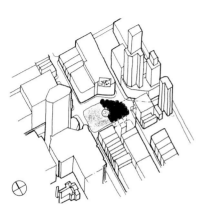

downtown residents, business associations, the local university, and a private developer. The new square connects with Dundas Street and Yonge Street. Yonge Street is Toronto's main street, and it is also the longest street in the world. Dundas Square has also been developed as a flagship project for a regeneration strategy for part of the Yonge Street corridor, specifically to assist in creating an urban entertainment centre, a role similar to that of Leicester Square in London's West End. The relationship between Yonge Street and Dundas Square will also be similar to that of 42nd Street and Times Square in New York, demonstrating the enduring theme of a main processional street connecting with a city square. Dundas Square has been designed to provide a world-class space for festivals and major city events, and it is now being used to market the city of Toronto around the world.

A complex pattern of land ownership around the site for Dundas Square was dealt with by the city authorities, which used public resources to buy out some owners, and used expropriation (compulsory purchase orders) when this failed. The use of expropriation has to be legally justified, and in the case of Dundas Square the decision to use it had to be defended at a quasi-judicial tribunal at the Ontario Municipal Board. It was successfully proved that the new square was appropriate and that it was a necessary improvement.

One of the key factors in facilitating the development of city squares as part of an urban design strategy is to secure control of strategic sites. When a partnership owns or controls key sites it can sell them to developers, attaching to them legally binding restrictive covenants to achieve the urban design objectives. For example, Oxford City Council in the UK successfully secured the development of Gloucester Green, a mixed-use town square with residential accommodation above commercial space, by producing a development brief for a site that the council already owned. Developers were then invited to interpret this brief in a commercially viable way, and to bid competitively for the contract to develop the site.

Community participation is essential in the production of these briefs and in the selection of winning master plans. If a partnership has no control over the necessary sites, and if a public-sector partner does not have compulsory purchase or expropriation powers, the partnership is in a weak position and more radical solutions have to be sought.

In the 1970s, the notion of planning gain gradually became established in the UK planning system. This provides a way of achieving urban design or planning objectives through a loose form of public–private partnership, without the need for public land ownership. Through planning gain, local authorities can require developers to undertake necessary improvement works off-site, or to receive funds for such improvement works, by way of planning conditions or legal agreements attached to planning consents. These additional requirements have to be reasonably related to the scheme for which a developer seeks planning consent. A local authority could therefore work in partnership to prepare development sites around a proposed new square, and could then ask the developers of these sites to pay something towards the creation of the new public space.

The city of Toronto paid for the creation of the new public space at Dundas Square itself, but raised funds through the use of 'bonusing money'. This is money paid by developers for the privilege of exceeding prescribed building heights or densities. However, with this approach (at least in theory), some areas of the city are suffering so that other parts can be improved.

Another approach is to encourage landowners to enter into a partnership and to provide their land in return for a share of the development profits. This can prevent the time-consuming and adversarial process of compulsory purchase.

Tax-related funding

In Europe, public-sector grants have been used in depressed areas to encourage private-sector development, but in the USA the taxation system is also used in a proactive way to finance urban design and renewal projects. The provision of tax incentives has become one of the most important regeneration tools in the USA, and they are largely used instead of grant schemes. The rules for 'tax implement financing' (TIF) differ from state to state, but the basic idea is the same. Part of the new revenue generated by property tax from development within a defined area is used to pay off bonds that finance other improvement works.[23] In the city of Chicago, TIF has been used as an effective urban regeneration tool. Chicago's first TIF district was established in 1984, and 44 were in place by 1997.

The TIF process involves the city authority designating a regeneration area and establishing a local partnership organisation, which then manages resources. The property taxes in the regeneration area are fixed at a low level to encourage investors to operate in the area. Once investment has been made, and the public realm has been improved, property values are likely to increase. Any increase in property taxes goes to the local partnership, rather than to the city hall. Through this approach, more money stays in the local area and the partnership can accumulate substantial funds for reinvestment. The system has resulted in a cycle of growth and has potential to assist in implementing urban design strategies that include exciting new public spaces.

Chicago's city planning department reported in July 1998 that an impressive leverage ratio had been achieved within their TIF areas, with six private-sector dollars being invested for every public dollar spent. (The overall public investment had been US$300 million, which had attracted a private investment of US$1.8 billion – the total investment was therefore US$2.1 billion.) Growth has continued, with many thousands of new dwellings being developed in Chicago's downtown district and edge of downtown, in areas where no private housing market had existed.

Another way of using the tax system to regenerate areas with a weak property market is to arrange for investors to receive property taxes directly from the partnership. In effect, these taxes can serve as revenue, providing some guarantee of a financial return. This compensates for the increased uncertainty and risk that developers take on when investing within a regeneration area. Similar to TIF areas, 'tax abatement districts' (TADs) have been established within cities in the USA under a 1997 law that allows cities to forgive taxes on a development for up to ten years. Both TIF and TAD initiatives have their critics, and it has been argued that they have been used in areas where the private sector would have invested regardless of the tax advantages. Notwithstanding this, the city of Chicago demonstrates that they can be effective and are relatively simple to operate. When TIF districts have been successful, there has usually been a powerful mayor figure who has provided the vision and leadership required to create partnerships between the public, private, and community groups.

Following the American model, the UK Government has introduced 'business improvement districts' (BIDs), funded by a compulsory improvement fund raised from the local business community. The focus for BIDs is on the management of the public realm in commercial centres, to provide facilities and services above those provided by local authorities. They could facilitate the longer-term funding required to develop and implement urban design strategies within commercial centres.

Phasing implementation

Once a regeneration partnership's organisational and management structures have been agreed, a funding plan is in place, and an urban design strategy has been produced with community support, consideration needs to be given to the phasing of implementation. The phasing plan for a major development scheme will probably be dependent on the release of funds during the life of the project – but there are other important considerations. For example, the phasing plan should aim to create a prestigious and marketable image as soon as possible, to inspire confidence and to develop market interest. The phasing plan also needs to ensure that a prestigious image is maintained on site during the life of the project.

If the main public spaces within a new development are built first, an impressive image can be created from the beginning. The public frontages that face onto these spaces can then follow soon after. When site hoardings are decorated with artist's impressions of the final development, they help to inspire confidence and interest in the development.

The phasing plan needs to consider how much new commercial and residential

DUKE OF YORK'S
Behind this hoarding
Cadogan is creating a
new square with public
access along with shops,
offices and homes.

Right. Innovative hoardings around a site in Chelsea in London generate interest by providing information about a planned new square.

floor space can be released onto the market without depressing property prices. This is where property and real estate expertise are crucial. If property prices fall, the whole project could be jeopardised. The phasing plan also needs to ensure that completed buildings can be occupied, and thereby bring in income, with minimum interference from the development of later phases. Implementing development in a logical sequence is especially important where it will take several years to complete the whole project. Investors need to be satisfied that they will not be occupying expensive premises on a building site.

COMMUNITY PARTICIPATION STRATEGIES

The identity of an area is most valuably characterised by its people, and as such the role of the community is particularly important in producing an urban design strategy. The support of local residents and business people is also essential if the strategy is to realise its full potential. Through working closely with local people and by regarding them as local experts, the local community may begin to adopt the strategy as its own. This could provide additional political support, enthusiasm, and motivation, all of which will assist in implementation. An inclusive approach will also increase the likelihood of the community being concerned about the maintenance and upkeep of the square once it has been developed.

There will be many social, economic, political, financial, and design reasons for considering alternative locations for new city squares and other flagship projects. When the public and private sectors work in partnership with the local community to produce an urban design strategy, this will help to increase understanding about the hierarchy of movement patterns and public spaces, and thereby ensure that investment is made where it will have the biggest impact.

The design and management of public space should, as far as is practically possible, be a democratic process. Developing a partnership approach with the local community will facilitate this and will probably increase the resources available to implement the strategy. When applying for funding from government or other sources, evidence of local public support for the project is likely to be required. For example, the UK Government expects its urban regeneration funds to be spent through local partnerships, which are required to 'encourage active involvement from all relevant interests in the private and public sectors, and in local voluntary and community organisations'.

One way of developing an urban design strategy that is responsive to community demands is to follow a cyclical process of 'inquiry by design'.[24] This approach has been used effectively in consultancy work at Oxford Brookes University.[25] Before this process can begin, the management structure of the organisation needs to be in place – be it a joint venture company, partnership committee, or some other form of partnership. The multidisciplinary professional team also needs to be in place with clearly defined individual responsibilities. With these key roles established the process starts with the professional team undertaking a public participation exercise, to establish what the local issues are.

Preliminary consultation exercises

One way to initiate an enthusiastic public response is to start with a completely blank page and ask people to produce wish lists, although care is required not to raise expectations unrealistically (with a resulting loss of credibility). Alternatively, people may prefer to have something to respond to. The outline summary of issues and objectives as discussed at the initial partnership meetings can serve to structure the debate. Through networking with local schools, residents, and business groups, events can be organised to motivate people into participating in the process of developing an urban design strategy. Public participation techniques have been developed to establish user demands, and a broad selection of media can be used to reach people, including public meetings, community forums, interviews, networking groups, television and radio, leaflets, newsletters, newspapers, public exhibitions, and participatory workshops. It will probably be appropriate to use

LOCAL EXPERTS   CONSULTANTS

THE SOLUTION

Above. The cyclical process of 'inquiry by design'[24]
(Courtesy of Dr John Zeisel.)

different techniques to reach different groups of people at various stages in the production of the strategy.

At participatory workshops, a simple technique to establish how people perceive the study area is to ask them to draw 'mental maps' of it, including all the streets, buildings, public places, and landmarks that they can remember. This will provide an indication of how legible the area is to them, and will indicate which areas have a positive image and which areas require improvement. Local people will know the area well, and through an approach that regards them as local experts an effective working relationship can be formed.

At the start of the process it is important to reach common agreement on the key urban design aims and objectives. This is crucial because the strategy and designs will be built to satisfy these objectives and they will help to ensure that people will not have to go back to first principles further down the line.

At the end of the initial public consultation exercise it should be clear what local people perceive to be the main weaknesses and strengths of their area, and what steps they consider appropriate to improve its identity. After the exercise the professional design team should produce sketch proposals that address the issues raised by the local community. Public spaces are so integral to urban character that they are very likely to be raised as a key issue. Proposals to create new and improved public spaces and interconnected streets may become one part of a broader strategy proposed by the professionals to regenerate the area.

Presentation of preliminary design proposals and second consultation exercise

Once the proposals have been sketched up and simple models made to illustrate ideas, a second public consultation exercise follows. This next stage begins with presentation of the design ideas and an explanation of how they relate to the issues raised during the first public consultation exercise. The second public consultation exercise also provides the community with the opportunity to respond to these design proposals, providing valuable feedback for the designers.

A focused approach is required, and members of the public are often keener to respond to ideas or options that are visually displayed in a way that can be easily understood. Three-dimensional drawings or models can be crucial to aid understanding of how two-dimensional plans will appear in reality. Presenting ideas in a three-dimensional form is particularly helpful when communicating ideas to people who are not design professionals. Computer technology can assist in presenting development proposals in an open and accessible way, and can help to generate public interest and involvement in the production of an urban design strategy and in the development of new city squares.

Computer packages are available that allow an accurate three-dimensional computer model of a site or context to be generated from architectural drawings, verified site survey information, and controlled photographic information. People using such computer systems can then manipulate viewpoints to see how a development would appear from different perspectives.

Once these computer models are in place, it is feasible that members of the public will be able to take a virtual-reality walk through proposed new environments from the comfort of their own homes or offices. Computer terminals can also be provided at public consultation events, with assistance on hand. People expect three-dimensional computer representations to be accurate, and therefore some form of verification of accuracy needs to be developed. To avoid misrepresentation and potential litigation, it is important that it is made clear how accurate the representations of reality are.

Traditionally constructed wooden or plastic models are also effective tools for illustrating design ideas, especially when they are produced in a robust way that allows people to interact with them. They are especially useful for audiences who do not want to use computers.

Rough perspective sketches are also helpful for demonstrating ideas. It can become tempting for designers to elaborate plans and drawings until they become precious works of art in themselves, but these become inflexible and often do not provide enough information about how the final product will look in a three-dimensional form. Similarly, it may be tempting to produce glossy promotional material, but this can look as if decisions have already been made, or as if designers are trying to sell their own vision rather than being open to community feedback. This kind of material is best produced at the end of the process, when all stakeholders are satisfied with the proposals.

The presentation of design proposals is followed by a second round of public consultation. The aim of the second round is to establish the response of the partnership and the local community to the sketch proposals.

Final design proposals and presentation

After the second public consultation stage, design ideas are worked up in a way that realistically reflects user demands. The final strategy, with all of its design proposals, can then be presented to the partnership, the local community, and city authorities for approval. If some of the ideas of the community proved to be unrealistic, it is important to clearly communicate the reasons why they cannot be implemented. If the process collapses due to lack of public support, further cycles of consultation and design response may have to be undertaken.

The strategy could encompass several different urban design and regeneration projects, with new public spaces meeting many of the strategy's objectives. When the strategy includes several development proposals it is helpful to package them into a single vision, perhaps with an easily identifiable logo, catch phrase, or mission statement, which can be easily understood and marketed. The fact that the objectives within a strategy are commonly agreed by a partnership board and through public participation will give the strategy the authority of the community and so provide a powerful aid to implementation. This will also help to secure a smoother ride for planning applications and other regulatory procedures that could otherwise result in lengthy delays, increase costs, and jeopardise the whole project.

Local residents and business people can become major stakeholders in the implementation of an urban design strategy – in the creation of new public spaces.

PUBLIC SPACE MANAGEMENT

Once a new square has been constructed, the management of the space within it will be instrumental to its success. City squares have always contained festivals and served as a collective gathering place. Today, the effectiveness of any management strategy that involves special events and festivals will depend on cooperation from the owners of buildings and space around a square. If there are many independent units located around a square, skilled negotiation will be required to gain the support of business and property managers. Bringing together different owners and interest groups in this way can help to strengthen community identity.

Public space managers

Organising events that generate activity within a square requires a skilled public space manager who can be accountable to a board representing the people that live and work in the area around a square. This manager can then become a key figure, responsible for providing a comprehensive management strategy and maintenance programme for a city square, and for fund raising.

The role of a manager will be more effective if they have been involved with the design and development of the square; they will then be more likely to know about its capacity to accommodate various functions. They will need to know how many people can be safely accommodated within the square, how loud a public address system can be before it intrudes upon surrounding residents and office workers, and how much load the paving within the square can bear (the latter determining the weight limit for delivery trucks and the weight of a stage that can be built upon the square).

A city square's manager can market the square as a venue for major events, and through this activity will be marketing the city itself. The manager should adopt a coordinating role, supervising licences for street entertainers, vendors, cleaners, and general maintenance. They need to ensure that there is easy access to the square for everyone, including the disabled, and that a perception of safety is maintained through crime prevention measures. The manager also needs to ensure that empty premises are filled quickly by liaising with property managers and retailers.

A management plan is likely to be easier to implement when the open space within a square is owned by a single organisation. A common scenario is when a city authority is the landowner, and they appoint a manager with specific responsibility for generating activity within its city squares. This is the case in Birmingham, UK, where the city council employs a town centre manager with general responsibility for the maintenance of the squares. This manager helps to coordinate teams which organise annual arts festivals that are held within the city squares.

Public events

Some kind of booking procedure is likely to be required for major events that are to be held within a city square, which can help to ensure that appropriate activities occur throughout the day and evening. It will be a reflection of the success of a square if there is a waiting list of groups and organisations that want to use the square for their events. Through accommodating local groups, the collective identity of the urban community can be enhanced.

In 1998, Birmingham held its first *Artsfest*, a programme of over 200 events, with 800 artists performing over a three-day period. The *Artsfest*, inspired by the *Uitmarkt* festival held in Amsterdam, is held within the city squares and surrounding theatres and galleries. One of the objectives of the festival is to break down the barriers

Below Right. The Duke of York Square, created in 2003 in Chelsea in London, is a public space that is owned and managed by a private landlord (the Cadogan Estate). (Courtesy of Adam Parker Photography.)

Below Left. Birmingham's squares are transformed into festival space every year. A temporary ice skating rink is shown here at Christmas time in Victoria Square.

between the arts so that people are encouraged to attend diverse events, ranging from classical ballet to modern bhangra music. The city squares are turned into stages and the connecting roads are closed to vehicles to help accommodate the crowds.

Similar festivals are organised within city squares around the world to promote local identity and social inclusion. In the USA, Seattle's *Out To Lunch* programme provides music, dance, and theatre every day between June and September in fourteen different squares and parks in the city centre. This event has been supported financially by the City of Seattle, city-centre businesses, the federal administration, and the American Federation of Musicians. A survey at four different events in different locations revealed that 87 per cent of people there had been introduced to a space that they had not been in before.[26] The event also attracts many thousands of visitors every year.

Several lessons have been learned by Seattle's *Out To Lunch* festival organisers. To ensure that stages and audiences do not impede pedestrian flows, lightweight folding chairs are used for audiences, with the first row of chairs already in place to define the preferred distance between the spectators and the performers. Amplification should not be too loud because the audience will stand too far away from the performers, leaving less space available for a crowd. To ensure a high attendance, events should be timed to coincide with workers' lunch breaks, typically from 12.00 to 2.00 p.m., and food should be provided. Highly visible and well-designed signs are important for publicising the festival events well in advance.

The Mayor of London marked the completion of the refurbishment of Trafalgar Square in 2003 by introducing *Summer in the Square*, a three-month programme of events that showcase the vast array of cultural activity to be found in London, the UK, and around the world. Chapter Two of this book describes how obstacles to pedestrian movement around Trafalgar Square have been removed, how the northern side of the square, in front of the National Gallery, has been pedestrianised, and how a new grand staircase has been centrally positioned to accommodate pedestrian desire lines (see the case study – *Strategy for World Squares*). New toilets, a cafe, and disabled lift access have also helped to create a useful and enjoyable place out of a space that previously served as a traffic island. Visitors to the square can now expect to see site-specific choreography, which is used to animate the new staircase. There is also street theatre and live music, as well as public talks on the history of the square and the surrounding monuments and institutions.

Food and vending

In his study of open spaces in Manhattan, William Whyte observed that a square with a food kiosk or outdoor cafe is much more likely to attract people, and that this has a multiplier effect.[4] Successful street vendors know where the most connected and sociable places are – their livelihoods depend upon them locating there. Good vendors have a part to play in generating activity within a city square, especially because the food and drink they sell attracts people. Other basic essentials, such as seats, bins, and public conveniences, should also be near to prime vending pitches.

When vendors sell specialist items that are not found in surrounding shops they complement the retail provision around a square. A well-located city square will be busy at lunchtime and vendors can offer a useful service to office and shop workers. These workers may not have the time or energy to go around large stores at lunchtime, when they are most likely to want to relax in a square. Vendors are also often welcomed by people waiting at public transport stops.

Care is required when vendors are directly competing with the permanent traders – shop traders will have higher overhead costs and are therefore likely to resent any unfair competition. The goodwill of the permanent business people is required for the effective management of the square. Vendors should usually sell items such as flowers, fruit, and vegetables, which add colour and fragrance, as well as hot snacks and newspapers.

The business activities and quality of vendors needs to be kept under the close control of a city square manager. This can be achieved through the issuing of licences, which provide controls over the location of vending pitches and can influence the

Right. Good vendors have a role to play in generating activity and providing colour, as shown by these flower stalls in a market square in Nice in France.

Left. A new cafe society has been created in Brindley Place, Birmingham.
Above. A new cafe in the Duke of York Square in London. (Courtesy of Adam Parker Photography.)

appearance of vending units, products, and service quality.

Vending pitches can be positioned to generate activity within any underused areas of a square, or in spaces that require greater surveillance. Locating vendors in trouble spots, for instance where drug dealing has become a problem, has been an effective way of reclaiming space from criminals. Clearly, though, pitches for vendors must be located where potential customers will use them and will feel safe, and as such they need to be within direct sight of pedestrian flows.

Old buildings

Where existing old buildings stand around a square, consideration should be given to retaining them so they can be put to viable uses that will generate activity. Owners of such buildings are more likely to have paid off their capital investment and can therefore accept lower rents than can owners of newer buildings. If a building requires improvements, the rent could be even lower. This presents an opportunity for accommodating businesses and organisations that could not normally afford a location within a main city square but which may provide unique attractions. These could include theatres or community halls, features that can promote local identity and satisfy local needs.

Monitoring performance

The success of a square's design and management strategy can be monitored and measured in terms of 'vitality' and 'viability'. For example, counts of the pedestrian flows within the square and of the yields of buildings around the square can be taken as business performance indicators. Where these figures have been recorded in the area around the square prior to its development or improvement, the square manager can compile statistics and make comparisons to see how the square has affected the locality. Analysis of these statistics will indicate whether or not the square has been a business success. Statistics need to be compiled on at least an annual basis to monitor the longer-term performance of the square.

A paper produced by the Oxford Institute referred to 'footfall' as 'a direct indicator of the vitality of shopping streets'.[27] Footfall, or counts of pedestrian flows, can also be used to assess the vitality of the city square. Any increase in pedestrian flows is likely to be reflected in an increase in retail property values.

The yield of prime commercial property indicates how attractive an area is to investors. Yield is the ratio of rental income to capital value, and is expressed in terms of the open market rents of a property as a percentage of the capital value. The higher the yield, the lower the rental income is valued, and vice versa. A high yield will be of concern to investors, indicating that rental income will be a poor return, and as a result of this the area may suffer from a lack of investment. Vacancy rates are also much used in assessing an area's economic health.

If a new city square is successful and local businesses are trading well, the yield value of property in the area will be kept low and confidence high. There is a danger that if rents rise too high they will restrict the kind of uses that can afford to locate around the square. Uses that can afford the highest rents, such as banks, insurance and real estate offices, often generate the least activity. The report *Vital and Viable Town Centres*, produced by the Urban and Economic Development Group for the then Department of the Environment (UK), provides a comprehensive analysis for assessing the economic health of a local centre.[28]

The kind of uses that can generate a great deal of community activity, such as cafes, restaurants, meeting halls, and theatres, often cannot afford high rents. One way to manage this problem is to include a specific policy in a statutory plan for the area that limits the planning consents that will be given for uses that do not generate community activity within a city square. This has the effect of restricting market rents and creates a more accommodating environment for vitality generating uses. This kind of market intervention requires research and monitoring to ensure that it is effective and will not have negative or unforeseen consequences.

The city square manager needs to maintain regular discussions with traders, business people, residents, and visitors to assess if their perceptions of the square have altered, or to establish whether the spatial requirements of different groups are likely to change.

Valuable partnerships can be formed between city authorities and local universities to monitor the long-term success of city squares and other city centre improvements. These are of educational value and can be cost effective when compared with consultants' fees. University departments are also likely to participate in longer-term analyses.

In Copenhagen in Denmark, the programme of improvements to streets and squares has since 1968 been subject to detailed survey work by researchers from the city's School of Architecture at the Royal Academy of Arts. This work has included extensive interviews with the city centre's users, and shows how improvement works have influenced behaviour patterns. The survey results have indicated how improvements to city squares have had positive benefits for local people, businesses, and visitors. These findings have helped to provide the authorities with the motivation to press on with a strategy to improve the city.

PERFORMANCE CHECKS: MAKING PLACE FROM SPACE

- Has a 'champion' been appointed who can lead the partnership and pull all stakeholders towards a shared vision? Has a project director been appointed who can secure delivery of the vision?

- Has a partnership body been established that has a clearly defined identity and is representative and able to build on the strengths of the public, private, and community sectors?

- Has a multidisciplinary professional team been formed whose members share the vision and have adequate experience?

- Has a contextual analysis been produced to aid decision making and does this explain in an accessible way how the study area fits together physically and socially?

- Has a local catchment area been identified and has demographic information been researched so the design can relate to potential user requirements?

- Has a creative approach been adopted in securing appropriate resources, including land, professional expertise, and finance?

- Has a community consultation strategy been produced to engage local people in the design process and to gain their support for change?

- Is a management structure in place to ensure the square is a pleasant and commercially viable place, and is monitoring to be undertaken to ensure the public space remains commercially competitive?

- Is the management regime accountable to local interests, and is social inclusion promoted through provision of services and by accommodating festivals and other special events?

CHAPTER TWO>

CHAPTER TWO
LOCATION AND MOVEMENT

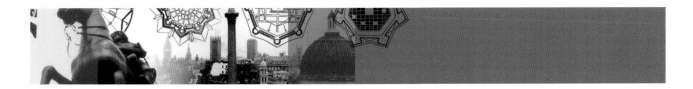

Some of the elements at the disposal of the designer are rhythmic arrangements of streets, the creation of a strong centre, and the disposition of open spaces.

Spiro Kostof, *The City Shaped*.[29]

Movement through the city is a crucial issue for any urban design strategy to understand. This is because the most urban activity, the highest densities of buildings, and the most prestigious city uses, tend to focus around the highest pedestrian flows. These are all essential ingredients for a city square. This chapter is concerned with principles for locating city squares in strategic locations, where they will knit with the surrounding urban area and be close to the hub of the movement network. Principles of access, legibility, movement, and servicing will also be addressed at a more site-specific level. The way in which movement patterns influence the city square and affect the wider urban area will be explored by focusing on a strategy to create 'World Squares' in London. This example, which focuses on Trafalgar Square, illustrates how a strategic urban design initiative can be used to adapt highway and transportation infrastructure in order to improve public space.

    The chapter will also show how the city authorities in Copenhagen, Denmark, have since 1962 been implementing a strategy within Copenhagen's streets and squares to improve the city by promoting walking. This example shows that when people move at a pedestrian pace they are more aware of the intrinsic qualities of their environment, and are therefore more concerned about the quality of the public realm. Increasing pedestrian freedom and improving the image of city squares has boosted tourism and economic confidence in Copenhagen's city centre. After experiencing the benefits associated with walking, many people have supported the further extention of controls on cars within the central area.

Understanding how people travel within an area is essential if a new public space is to be located effectively. Questions to be addressed include:

- to what extent do people walk, cycle, drive, or use public transport?
- what is the preferred mode of transport for different groups within the study area?

If the layout of the block structure or the design of the street network within a study area does not facilitate walking, or any other preferred mode of sustainable transport, consideration needs to be given to removing barriers and, possibly, to providing new routes and connections. As such, an urban design strategy needs to be closely integrated with highway and transportation policy.

A guiding principle for transportation within a study area is that different modes of transport are accommodated as long as they do not unreasonably prejudice the interests of other users of the public realm. Freedom of choice should be maintained for effective movement around an urban area, but with a bias towards sustainable means of transport – in particular, it is important to ensure that walking is an attractive and viable option.

For several decades highway design and maintenance has been undertaken in the UK in accordance with centrally determined rules and regulations, with little regard to the contextual qualities of specific streets and squares. As a result, unsightly signs, poor junction designs, overlarge lamp columns, and complicated staggered pedestrian crossings surrounded by lines of guard rails blight many public spaces. Even where schemes based upon local interpretation have been implemented, there has often been a confusing and random application of materials, with little evidence of a clear design rationale. Principles for the design of highway and traffic management systems are therefore touched on later in the chapter.

The way that public transport interchanges can be incorporated into urban design strategies for better public spaces will also be discussed to show how they can enhance the image of the city and improve the efficiency of transportation.

SPATIAL ORGANISATION

The wider urban structure and resulting movement patterns around potential sites for squares need to be assessed as part of the contextual analysis within an urban design strategy. The kind of questions that need to be addressed include whether there are any underused parts of the city or fragmented patterns of movement due to physical barriers that need to be removed or bridged. The image of the city can often be enhanced by improving connections between pedestrian flows. Urban structure, or morphology, refers to the layout of blocks of development and the resulting pattern of streets, open spaces, and buildings. Urban structure has the greatest influence on movement patterns in the city.

A primary requirement for a city square is a location at the junction of busy pedestrian flows – a well-connected location can then encourage a lively mix of uses. However, the public open spaces within many developments influenced by modernist planning and architecture are devoid of life because they are poorly located, and because the zoning of separate land uses results in single-use developments, be it housing or offices. These single-use areas contain buildings that are unoccupied for large parts of the day or night – office areas, for example, are left empty when workers go home in the evening. This often results in a lack of natural surveillance and problems with crime. (See Jane Jacobs' *The Death and Life of Great American Cities.*[2])

Research presented by Hillier and Hanson in their book *The Social Logic of Space*[30] reveals that the influence of the urban structure, essentially the streets and the blocks between them, has a fundamental influence upon patterns of movement. They claim that the layout of the urban structure is the most important factor in planning pedestrian movement, and as such this needs to be addressed before considering issues of building density or use:

Our research has shown that spatial organisation, over and above any effects due to the location of facilities and population density, has a crucial effect on the way people move through an urban area, and therefore on the way people become automatically aware of each other.

Bill Hillier and Julienne Hanson.[31]

(See also Refs 32 and 33 for more information on this subject.)

The way that a new city square connects to surrounding districts, and to the city as a whole, will be crucial to its success. The structure of the wider urban area can be analysed from a good base map (Ordnance Survey in the UK), a small scale of about 1:1,250 is ideal. This will reveal the block structure and pattern of voids in-between, which together define the location and shape of the streets and open spaces. The blocks, streets, and open spaces control the pattern of people moving through the urban area. An appropriate site for a city square will be well-connected, and accessible to many people.

The degree of movement within any square is dependent upon how well connected its site is to the surrounding urban area. For example, a square that is physically connected to strategic main streets and to other public spaces that bring people in to the city from its various parts will be highly accessible in the context of the settlement as a whole. For a new square to realise the status of the main public open space within the city, a location with a high degree of access is required – it needs to be at the centre of the city's movement network.

The typical spatial order within many traditional European cities is based on a 'deformed' grid pattern of perimeter blocks. This block structure is often good for legibility and for a clear visual structuring of the urban area because it results in a continuous chain of open spaces, through streets, and squares. When travelling through this chain of open spaces, sight lines are sometimes restricted and at other times extended due to the irregular arrangement of the building blocks and building lines. There will be wider and narrower sections of open space, and shorter and longer perspective views down streets. These views are more irregular than with a precise geometric grid, and often provide pedestrians with memorable glimpses of squares, buildings, and public works of art.

When axial sight lines are drawn on a base map along open stretches of streets and public spaces, they indicate the extent of open vision and demonstrate how visually permeable the area is. They show how visible a square would be for a pedestrian approaching from the surrounding streets. This visibility plays an important part in determining how accessible a square is. Hillier and Hanson refer to this process as 'axiality' and it forms part of their 'space syntax' theory[32].

The space syntax theory developed by Hillier and Hanson in the late 1970s enables the physical permeability of the urban layout to be objectively recorded, and once this has been done the accessibility of a given site can be calculated numerically. This information can be used to give a precise value of relative 'depth' or 'shallowness' for any location being considered for a new square. This is a complex but useful mathematical tool, which can help to ensure that a site for a new city square is well-connected and accessible.

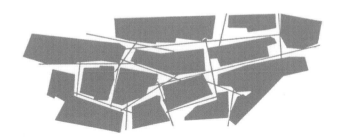

Right. Axial sight lines drawn along streets and squares in-between urban blocks in a typical European deformed grid layout. Through following the sight lines it is possible to count how many changes of direction are required to find a site from an arrival point. (Courtesy of Professor Bill Hillier/Space Syntax Limited.)

In space syntax theory, when it is necessary to pass through many indirect and inconvenient spaces in order to reach a site, the urban structure is described as having 'depth'. If the urban layout has a lot of depth, the chances are that many inconvenient changes of direction will have to be taken to find the main square, and there will be a lack of direct routes to it. A square located in an area with a lot of depth is unlikely to be very accessible, and there will be little choice in the number of routes that can be taken to find it. To improve this situation, urban surgery may be required to create new routes, and it may be necessary to consider a more accessible arrangement of buildings, streets, and blocks.

Our research suggests that the key difference in urban quality between spaces lies partly in how well the spaces are integrated with their surroundings. By analysing the relative depth and ascribing a numerical value to each space, we can get a picture of the relative integration of each space.

Bill Hillier and Julienne Hanson.[31]

When the urban layout includes many connections that are clear and direct, and when there are many alternative routes, Hillier and Hanson refer to the urban structure as being 'shallow'. An appropriate site for a city square would be within a surrounding urban structure that is axially shallow. Such a structure of streets and building blocks could typically be of the traditional European deformed grid pattern, it could also be of the more formal regular grid pattern associated with many cities in the USA, most graphically by Manhattan Island in New York. These grid layouts are permeable and accessible – they make it relatively easy to unravel the hierarchy of streets and to locate central locations for a new city square.

Hillier and Hanson refer to the width of any open void space between the building blocks as 'convexity' – a two-dimensional extension off an axial line of vision. The different uses and human activity that can be seen along these axial and convex sight lines determine how interesting and safe the streets are perceived to be on approach.

LEGIBILITY

Many modern cities have developed into an amorphous urban sprawl where we no longer expect to see the clear defining features, such as city walls, gates, or processional ways, that helped to structure the whole city. Kevin Lynch's *The Image of the City* [13] is useful for defining urban legibility, in terms of paths, nodes, landmarks, views, vistas, edges, and districts, as discussed in the Introduction (also see Appendix I). These elements help to structure the built environment in a meaningful way. While it is difficult to physically define the boundaries of a vast modern city, by creating a legible centre with a strong identity, urban design principles are established which can then be modelled in lesser centres and along routes across the city.

An appropriate site for a city square is one that is within an urban structure that offers a choice of routes, one that is both physically and visually permeable. Urban layout is the primary consideration in understanding movement patterns and in creating appropriate sites for city squares, but architectural design and public art can also be used to emphasise the location of a square and to ensure there are legible links to it from the surrounding city. Bill Hillier, who was jointly responsible for the space syntax theory, states that good spatial design for a city square means at least three things: [34]

- a good square has to relate well to patterns of movement
- it has positions within it with multidirectional strategic views, in proportion to the scale of the square and along lines of potential movement into and through the square
- the provision of facilities has to take into account the above two factors, by creating places to stop from which people could see, close to, but not on, the lines of movement.

If both the layout of streets and the arrangement of landmark features lead people to a main square, an urban area will have a clear focal point that can be used to strengthen its identity. This kind of urban form can be seen dramatically in surviving European fortified towns, for example in the Tuscan hill town of Todi, where the main square, the Piazza del Popolo, remains upon the site of an ancient Roman forum.

These fortified medieval towns are relatively small and are densely developed – they can often be seen in their totality when they are located on higher ground (for defence reasons). In Todi's Piazza del Popolo, towers rise to give architectural definition to the corners of the square, and principal buildings rise up to an elevated level where they appear dominant and solid. The mayor's palace, located at the southern end of the square, represents the power of state, while the cathedral stands opposite and dominates the whole square and town. Grand flights of stairs take the design to a different level, there is excitement in their ascent as they afford new perspectives and open views.

Useful urban design principles can be taken from these surviving medieval and early Renaissance settlements. The tallest buildings in Italian cities from this period usually mark the location of the main square, while lesser towers mark the smaller neighbourhood squares. This hierarchy of interconnected squares results in an organic kind of urban structure.

The Piazza San Marco in Venice provides the clearest example of a city square with dominant architectural elements, such as towers that are echoed at a diminished scale in the smaller public spaces throughout the city. This hierarchy of towers provides a design unity through the city as a whole. Bacon states 'The many church towers and spires recall but never dominate the Campanile of San Marco's'[35].

Left. The Grand Canal in Venice functions as a processional route which enters the Piazza San Marco with a momentous sense of arrival.

The Campanile of San Marco is just under 100 m in height, and as such it has served as a beacon, not just for those within the city but also for seafarers. The tower is crowned with a large gilded statue of an angel, which rotates with the wind. The great square beneath it is the only public open space in Venice to be called a 'piazza', the many lesser squares are called 'campi', which again reinforces the sense of a hierarchy.

Venice also includes a processional way, the Grand Canal, which is lined by Renaissance palaces and provides a triumphal sense of arrival into the central Piazza San Marco. The relationship of the processional way and the central square, the fairly constant height of ordinary buildings, the densely developed narrow streets, and the hierarchy of public spaces, all help to create a legible city with a strong identity.

ROAD SPACE

Innovative public space improvement schemes in London, such as at Trafalgar Square and Kensington High Street, have shown that pedestrian and vehicular movement can both be accommodated in a way that is safe, convenient for all users, and visually attractive. In both cases, a well-structured partnership and project management approach was adopted, and highway design issues tackled by examining the evidence on the ground rather than slavishly following a rule book.

A guiding principle for street improvements along Kensington High Street has been 'less is more' – for example, a simple palette of the highest quality materials has been used. The Royal Borough of Kensington and Chelsea uses the following statement from William Morris to underpin its philosophical approach: 'Have nothing in your houses which you do not know to be useful or believe to be beautiful'. The Council insists that everything placed on its streets must add to its surroundings by serving an essential purpose or by adding beauty. Its *Streetscape* guide,[36] published in 2004, includes the following main principles for good streetscape:

Above. Kensington High Street, new keep left sign with uplighter. (Courtesy of Royal Borough of Kensington and Chelsea/Project Centre Ltd/Woodhouse.)

- ▓ reducing clutter
- ▓ use of a simple palette of high-quality materials
- ▓ respecting and enhancing local character
- ▓ use of simple, clean designs
- ▓ coordinating design and colour
- ▓ maintaining the existing and improved environment
- ▓ preserving historic paving and street furniture.

Implementing this approach at Kensington High Street has led to the removal of street clutter created by uncoordinated street furniture, varying paving materials, convoluted pedestrian crossing points and junction designs, and highway signs. All unnecessary pedestrian guard railing has been removed along the High Street and the standard plastic highway signs have been replaced with low-level stainless steel loop signs.

The graceful lines of Kensington High Street's 1930s department stores provided the cue for the choice of the new street furniture. The new stainless steel lamp columns form an important architectural feature of the scheme. Many other items, such as traffic lights and litterbins, are physically attached to them in a visually integrated way. The lamps provide white light, which allows real colours to be seen at night, and are designed to avoid light pollution. A separate footway lamp is included, which better relates to the scale of a pedestrian and includes a softer white light.

Pavements along Kensington High Street have been widened and are realigned to conform to building lines. This has resulted in a safer and more attractive pedestrian environment. Pedestrian crossings have been redesigned in an innovative way that avoids all unnecessary clutter. Pedestrians now have the opportunity to cross the road in a single movement, rather than being penned in between guard railing on islands in the middle of the carriageway. People in wheelchairs no longer have their view of on-coming traffic obscured by pedestrian guard railing.

Potential conflict between pedestrians and vehicles has been overcome by coordinating the timing of traffic signal lights along the whole High Street to ensure that vehicle flows move smoothly but do not have time to build up excessive speed. The lessons learned from Kensington High Street are now being applied across all of the public spaces within the Royal Borough.

Above. A new lamp column on Kensington High Street, designed to accommodate traffic signals and other street furniture, such as litter bins. (Courtesy of Royal Borough of Kensington and Chelsea/Project Centre Ltd/ Woodhouse.)

WALKING

A modern boy travels a hundred miles with less sense of liberation and pilgrimage and adventure than his grandfather got from travelling ten.

C. S. Lewis, Surprised by Joy.[37]

The benefits of providing pedestrians with more road space include reduced air pollution and noise and less danger from fast moving vehicles. These all improve the quality of public space and increase pedestrian freedom to move across it. The benefits are often multiplied when there is a wider pedestrian network linking squares and streets that attract large numbers of people. When busy roads bound three or four sides of a square, it becomes difficult to create a public space with a pedestrian character. This is because the roads act as physical barriers against pedestrians entering the square, and result in noise and pollution. Such spaces are often landscaped and become attractive traffic islands, but rarely successful city squares.

Given the large areas of open space taken up by roads and vehicles, special consideration needs to be given to the design of public open space when cars are taken away from it. Particular care is required to ensure that streets and squares do not appear empty or devoid of life. Some caution is therefore required with total pedestrianisation because if pedestrian flows are low, public space may be perceived as being unsafe and can then require expensive security measures. To prevent this from occurring, the design of routes within and around the city square need to feed off the existing pedestrian flows.

While motor vehicles within a city centre can cause a hostile environment for pedestrians, people within vehicles can represent activity and provide a sense of surveillance over the public realm. Cars and trucks also allow for bulk deliveries, which can keep down transport costs and, consequently, the price of goods. Careful planning is therefore required to ensure that a strategy for pedestrianisation will deliver more beneficial effects than harmful ones.

The effects of pedestrianisation on the servicing of businesses also needs to be carefully considered. High pedestrian flows are essential for business, but retailers may object to pedestrianisation schemes if they mean that passing trade from people in cars is lost. Pedestrian flows also need to be high enough throughout day and evening to provide activity and surveillance to ensure that pedestrianised streets and squares are perceived to be safe. If the use of motor vehicles is to be restricted in an area, effective planning is required to ensure that adequate alternative means of transport are available. For example, effective public transport is required, together with direct pedestrian and cycle routes that are separated from any fast moving vehicles. Secure cycle parking located at main destination points is necessary, and employers need to provide shower facilities if workers are to cycle to work.

As city squares are essentially for people, rather than motor vehicles, the management or redirection of traffic may be necessary to create a pedestrian character. As already explained, it is crucial for the vitality of a square that it is accessible to high pedestrian flows within the surrounding area. However, the number of trips made by walking has continued to decrease in many modern cities, just as car traffic has continued to increase, with a resulting negative effect upon the public realm.

A research report completed in 1998 by Carmen Hass-Klau for the UK Government[38] revealed that the percentage of trips made by walking has generally declined over recent years, both in the UK and in mainland Europe. In the UK there was a 7 per cent drop in walking within the major urban metropolitan areas between 1985/6 and 1993/5. By 1995 only 29 per cent of journeys were being made on foot. The report states that there has been a tendency to replace walking as a means of transport with car trips, rather than using a more environmentally sustainable alternative.

A number of surveys have been undertaken in Germany and Austria, before and after pedestrianisation of streets and squares. The pedestrian counts were taken over many years and revealed significant increases in the number of walkers in pedestrianised areas.[3] Within Groningen city centre in the Netherlands, a restrictive transport policy has increased the percentage of trips made by walking, cycling, and public transport, at the expense of the car. In 1976, 35 per cent of all trips were made by car, and by 1985 this had been reduced to 22 per cent. There was a 1 per cent increase in use of public transport, a 5 per cent increase in cycling, and a 7 per cent increase in walking, with an improved, people-friendly, environment for everyone in the city centre.[39] In Goteborg in Sweden, a pedestrianisation scheme reduced the overall mean carbon dioxide level from 30 ppm to 5 ppm.[40]

In Copenhagen in Denmark, the main streets and city squares have been gradually pedestrianised since 1962 – this city provides an example of the benefits of creating a pedestrian-friendly city centre. Before 1962 all of the streets and public squares in Copenhagen's city centre were regularly congested with vehicular traffic, and all of the historic squares were used as car parks. The first street to be pedestrianised was the main commercial street, Strøget, which is the most connected city street. As soon as Strøget became free of traffic, it began to serve a new role as a street for promenading and for street entertainment. In the summer months the 11 m wide street became filled to capacity with people. Strøget links two important city squares, Kongens Nytorv to the east, which serves as the major public transport node, and Rådhuspladsen to the west, which is the central town hall square, and also serves as a public transport node and major events space.

Back in 1962, the proposal to pedestrianise Copenhagen's main street met with great hostility, especially from a sceptical press, who thought that pedestrian squares were only appropriate in sunny southern climates. However, the city council has continued to implement a programme of selective pedestrianisation.

The basic network of pedestrian streets was established by 1973, by which time the five most important pedestrian links within the city centre were either totally free of traffic, or had pedestrian priority on the carriageway and pavement. Once the main pedestrian links were in place, Copenhagen's city council spent the following years pedestrianising the city's central squares. In every year between 1962 and 1996 some additional pedestrian space was created in the city. During this period there was a sixfold increase in the area of pedestrianised space. By 1996 there were 96,000 m^2 of pedestrian outdoor public space in the city centre, and 67 per cent of this was within 18 city squares.

The fact that the pedestrianisation programme has been carefully phased over many years has helped to limit opposition. People have been able to experience the benefits of creating people places, and they have supported applying the same principles in other parts of the city. The outdoor cafes in the city squares are now well used, even during the cold winter months – when blankets are provided to keep customers warm! (See Ref. 7).

Pedestrian circulation

When a site is already used by the public, their movement through the space and behaviour within it will provide valuable clues about how the circulation space should be designed. The design of circulation space for pedestrian movement within a square should be based on analysis of the shortest routes between the square's access points, including access to important public buildings. Special attention needs to be given to any major attraction or drop-off point, and especially for a public transport stop or interchange.

Most well-connected city squares will have to accommodate not only peak rush hour pedestrian flows, but also people who will be passing through the space at a more leisurely pace. There will also be people accessing the uses and services within the square, such as shops, banks, museums, cafes, seating, or viewing areas, etc. Accommodating these different movement patterns and walking paces will have a significant influence on the design of the square, and its subspaces (see also Chapter Three, and Cooper Marcus and Francis, page 30[3]).

When considering how people will access a city square, and how they will circulate around the space within it, it is helpful to first consider where the arrival points into the square are, or where they could be created. To maximise activity and urban vitality, there need to be several well-connected arrival points that link

Above. Copenhagen's strategy for a sequence of pedestrianised streets and squares has helped to transform a city that was previously dominated by cars. (Courtesy of Jan Gehl and Lars Gemzøe.)

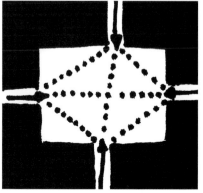

Above. Circulation space can be designed by providing direct connections between access points around a square.

Left. The area beside a busy pedestrian flow is ideal for sitting, resting, and 'people watching', as shown in this Manhattan street.

the square with the surrounding pedestrian flows. The arrival points into a square can be marked on a base plan and ranked according to their depth or shallowness and according to their rates of pedestrian flow. The links that have the highest number of pedestrian connections will probably be the most strongly connected to the surrounding urban area. (For an effective methodology, see *Responsive Environments* by Bentley *et al*., page 16[12].) Circulation routes can then be designed through the square to link these arrival points, and any other major access points into buildings.

If people are to be encouraged to enter a city square, there needs to be clear visual continuity from the streets that feed into it. There is a discussion on the design of the transition from street to square, and on creating legible gateways, in Chapter Three.

There is a tendency for pedestrian flows to remain in the middle of the space allocated to it, whether on a pavement or a flight of steps. The human activity

Above. 'People watching' beside a busy pedestrian flow in London.

Above Right. Ramped areas can be carefully integrated with steps to provide for attractive and dignified disabled access, as shown here at Brindley Place in Birmingham.

within a square is the major attraction and so the edges of the pedestrian flows become excellent places for people watching. These edges should therefore be designed for sitting and observing.

Pedestrians can be guided through the square by physical design techniques, for example through the positioning of walls and planters, strong texture changes (including the use of cobbles), or through a change of levels – the use of colour alone is not likely to be effective in directing people. A very simple palette of materials is usually more successful than an assortment of paving types. Wherever possible, it is best to accommodate natural pedestrian desire lines.

Steps are often proposed to provide access into parts of a site where there is a significant change in levels. While steps can provide an appealing vertical depth, and climbing them to observe the panorama of activity within the square can be a delight, they can also act as barriers to natural pedestrian flows if they are inconveniently located. Climbing steps takes longer than walking along a gradient, therefore steps can be an obstacle to pedestrian flows. Steps also pose a particular problem for people in wheelchairs, parents with buggies, the old, the very young, and the visually impaired, all of who are entitled to unrestricted access into the city square.

One solution in dealing with different gradients is to imaginatively shape the earth and thereby provide access for all without the need for steps or ramps. If it is decided that steps should be included, either for practical or aesthetic reasons, ramped areas can be carefully integrated into the design of steps. This requires the input of a skilled designer, especially as ramps take up to seven times more space than steps.

An effective way to ensure that steps can be clearly seen is to design the treads with an overhang, so that they project out 20 mm beyond the riser. This creates a distinctive shadowing effect on the riser, while the tread remains lit. This visual distinction is especially helpful when the tread and the rise are of the same colour and material. Lighting can also be included on the riser to ensure individual steps are clearly visible. Slippery surfaces are obviously dangerous and need to be avoided.

PUBLIC TRANSPORT INTERCHANGES

Locations where large numbers of the travelling public are passing through, e.g. between international, regional, and local connections, usually have great potential for development as major public spaces. Airports often have rail links connecting with city railway stations and these stations can form the main transport gateway into a city. As increasing numbers of people are likely to travel by plane and train, transport interchanges are required to provide smooth connections, and to be well integrated into the fabric of the city. If different modes of sustainable transport are located together at a transport interchange, with a railway station, bus station, and cycle and car parking, people can switch from one mode of transport to another and large areas of the city become accessible to them. Main city squares should ideally be less than 400 m (a ten-minute walk) from such interchanges.

Although business communications can be conducted to some extent through the internet, fax, and telephone, there is still a need for face-to-face contact, and today there is much more flexibility in choosing when and where this occurs. When people travel long distances for a meeting it is convenient for them to have easy access to a stimulating environment close to their point of arrival. Consequently, some railway stations and airports are becoming destination points in their own rights. While many transport interchanges provide connections between international, regional, and local modes of transport, they do not always integrate the structures and people associated with this travel into a legible, urban sense of place.

During a day at an international railway station there are likely to be thousands of people passing through, some of who may need a place to shop, eat, rest, or to do business. These people can represent the seeds for urban regeneration as they generate the activity that can result in dynamic new city squares. In France, the development of the TGV railways was originally seen as a catalyst for urban regeneration, although in reality it has had mixed results due to the lack of a coordinated strategy. However, the French railway company, SNCF, recently recognised the commercial potential of railway stations, and they have identified 45 stations that could become the focal points of redevelopment initiatives. It has been realised that property around a railway station has a worth directly proportional to the success of the transport node.[41]

In the city of Nîmes in France, new TGV connections have been integrated with proposals for a new city square and with other forms of public transport to create a transport interchange and an impressive sense of arrival.

If a railway station is designed to open on to a city square, it adds dramatically to the status of the space. It becomes a place for meetings, exhibitions, and a diversity of uses that say 'welcome to this city'. The square can provide travellers with easy access to all of the services they need in a quality urban environment. The square draws people out of the station so they can directly experience the city and add to its vitality. While many cities already have impressive public spaces at their main railway stations (as in Copenhagen, Amsterdam, and Toronto), other major railway stations provide access into a no-man's-land of traffic junctions and pedestrian subways. In London, there is great potential and need for an urban design strategy to improve the traffic-ridden nodes around its splendid Victorian railway stations, and to improve the spaces that link the stations with the surrounding city.

Below. New transport interchange and public space for Nîmes railway station in southern France.

Below Right. Saint Pancras Railway Station in London dates from 1866–8, it includes a dramatic clear span of 210 m which helps to provide an impressive gateway into London. The effect is diminished by a neglected public realm outside the station.

SERVICING

To reduce the number of vehicles on or around a square, buildings should ideally be serviced from their rears – this will also reduce the visibility of loading bays and service doors. Where the layout of the urban structure is made up of perimeter blocks, the most rational use of space may be to arrange service areas within the inner parts of these blocks. All buildings within the block can then be serviced from this single area. It helps to maintain the continuity of frontages onto a square if the service area is entered from an adjacent street rather than being directly off the square itself. If an entry point must be off the square, it should be as discrete as possible, perhaps with a well-designed vehicular gateway that is framed within a building frontage.

Prohibiting service vehicles from a public square improves the square's image and pedestrian freedom. Many urban centres have time restrictions on vehicular servicing arrangements, although these are sometimes poorly enforced. Restricting the size of service vehicles may be a further step in creating a people-friendly environment. In Venice in Italy good use is made of the canals for delivering heavy goods, and when streets and squares are located away from a canal, hand-pushed trolley carts are used to deliver heavy goods. These trolleys cause little nuisance and have potential to be used in other locations, especially when short distances have to be covered across busy pedestrian spaces.

Left. A service bay located within a block, with access from a side street.

Far Left. A pedestrian-friendly way of delivering bulky goods in Venice is to use trolleys that take goods from boats.

CASE STUDY
STRATEGY FOR WORLD SQUARES

Much of central London has an urban structure consisting of an irregular network of streets and squares. The result is a legible built environment with interesting architectural compositions, views, and vistas — but the city has also suffered from accommodating vehicular traffic.

Trafalgar Square, located at the heart of central London, was developed in the 1820s as an integral part of the urban design vision of John Nash. His plan was to connect two royal parks in a way that would enhance a large part of central London, and ensure that London was perceived as one of the finest cities in the world. The historic processional route of Whitehall leads directly off Trafalgar Square to the south and connects with Parliament Square. Parliament Square is enclosed by the Houses of Parliament and by Westminster Abbey, which have been designated by UNESCO as a World Heritage Site. Westminster clock tower, housing Big Ben, rises from the Houses of Parliament and acts as a landmark that closes an important vista looking south from Trafalgar Square. The combined effect of the spaces, buildings, and views results in one of the most powerful images of London.

The World Squares initiative focuses on Trafalgar Square and provides a useful case study for showing the kind of movement issues that need to be addressed to create a pedestrian-friendly city square. Before examining how the World Squares strategy has been developed, it is useful to present something of the history and layout of Trafalgar Square and its surroundings.

Trafalgar Square and its surroundings

Trafalgar Square occupies a politically charged spot at the heart of London. It demonstrates the primary importance of location, and also of getting the dimensions of the open space right. Although the buildings around the square have often been redeveloped, the public space has continued to serve in its role as the main square for London and the United Kingdom for almost two hundred years.

It was just off the site of Trafalgar Square that Renaissance architecture first established itself in London in 1619, when the Banqueting House was erected in

Left. The view from London's National Gallery looking south to Nelson's Column and to the clock tower of Big Ben beyond. The clock tower closes the vista down the processional route of Whitehall.

Above. War veterans march along the processional route of Whitehall, which links Trafalgar Square with Parliament Square, at the political heart of London .

Whitehall to the design of Inigo Jones. The Banqueting House is especially important in urban design terms because it provided the impetus for King James I to order an ambitious plan for the rebuilding of Whitehall to reflect the grandeur of this new stone building. The Banqueting House also helped Inigo Jones to secure a commission from the Earl of Bradford to design the Covent Garden Piazza. This was built between 1631 and 1638, on the garden of a convent that had been confiscated by Henry VIII, and became England's first formal square – Covent Garden continues to be one of London's most successful public spaces.

Whitehall itself is a symbolic street, which functions as a well-connected processional way linking Trafalgar Square and Parliament Square. The prominence of these spaces within the hierarchy of London's streets is reflected in the status of the buildings around them. Parliament Square is surrounded by the most prestigious buildings in London, from which the nation's secular and spiritual lifes are governed.

It was about two hundred years after Inigo Jones designed the Banqueting House that John Nash, still inspired by the principles of Renaissance design, developed his vision to restructure a large part of the West End of London. His vision would include a new square at the heart of the capital city. Nash's

Above. Traffic used to completely dominate Trafalgar Square – one of London's most symbolic public spaces was reduced to functioning as a traffic island.

Above Right. Trafalgar Square continues to attract many tourists, but now it also facilitates the daily movement patterns of ordinary Londoners.

proposals also included a monumental new route, Regent's Street – now one of London's principal shopping streets – to connect Regent's Park and Green Park. He proposed a direct link off Regent's Street to a monumental new public space, Trafalgar Square, which would be connected to London's other primary routes.

The task was enormous as the whole area was already densely developed, and held by a variety of different landowners. Nash's vision was eventually implemented – almost completely. It resulted in Trafalgar Square being built in the 1820s, and it soon became a symbolic heart for the city, the nation, and the British Empire. The site of Trafalgar Square has excellent connections with its surroundings, standing at the junction of London's most connected streets, including Charring Cross, Whitehall, and the Strand. The square is located at a node in the centre of London's road network. This centrality is marked by the fact that all UK traffic road signs giving the distance to London are measured to the centre of Trafalgar Square.

Trafalgar Square plays a prominent part in the life of the nation primarily because of its location and size. It provides a focal point where national demonstrations are held, and it also contains some of the nation's most important statues and monuments. As such it may be regarded as a 'state' space.

Improving pedestrian movement

Until recently, the legibility of Trafalgar Square and its surroundings was marred by vehicular traffic – in effect it was one of London's busiest traffic islands. This traffic was a serious barrier to pedestrian flows and Londoners tended not to cross the square, but would rather go on lengthy detours around it. Tourists and visitors to London were usually the only people with the determination to cross the four lanes of traffic required to enter the square, and they would congregate within certain parts of the square in large numbers.

The UK Government and the Mayor of London have recognised the potential of Trafalgar Square to provide a positive image for London, and resources have been allocated for an ambitious project marketed as 'World Squares'. This has focused on the processional route of Whitehall and on Parliament Square, as well as Trafalgar Square. An initial partnership was formed to produce a strategy and master plan to guide the implementation of the project. This included eight organisations, and the lead, which was initially taken by the local authority, Westminster City Council, passed to the new Mayor of London. The other partners include relevant government offices, English Heritage, and public transport companies.

The British architect Sir Norman Foster was appointed as consultant for the project, and his multidisciplinary team coordinated production of a master plan for the partnership. This master plan performs as an urban design and transport strategy to aid implementation of the project.

Bill Hillier (who was jointly responsible for the space syntax theory discussed earlier in this chapter) made the observation that Trafalgar Square was used almost exclusively by tourists and that Londoners walked around the edges of the square. He observed that the tourists were required to cross wide roads and to incur long delays at pedestrian crossings, or to cross dangerously and illegally. Most successful city squares facilitate natural pedestrian movement across space, but this was not the case with Trafalgar Square. There were several reasons for the failings of the square. Removing all of the existing vehicular traffic was considered not to be a viable option – as Bill Hillier stated: 'Removing the traffic would not in itself lead to the square "working" for all its potential constituencies'. A deeper analysis of the location and movement was required.

To remedy the problems of the site, and to facilitate an appropriate enhancement scheme, Bill Hillier's team recommended that Trafalgar Square must be used for normal pedestrian movement, as well as for tourists and local people to stop and rest in. To do this, the people that live and work in the surrounding area need to be able to walk across the square as part of their everyday lives.

Above. The steps located at the corners of Trafalgar Square were inconveniently located, away from pedestrian desire lines, leaving large areas of the square unused.

Below. An historic statue of King Charles I dating from 1675, located on one of London's most symbolic spots, but which served as a small traffic island.

Bottom. The new central staircase, aligned with the National Gallery and pedestrian desire lines.

Trafalgar Square consists of two main levels: the upper one fronting the National Art Gallery to the north, and the lower level to the south, beside the processional route of Whitehall. There were two flights of steps between the two levels, positioned at the eastern and western corners of the square. The location of these steps was inappropriate because they did not accommodate any natural pedestrian movement desire lines. The result was that the sharp change in levels, and the inappropriately positioned steps, restricted pedestrian movement between the upper and lower sides of the square. Although there are spectacular views down Whitehall from the upper level, this part of the square was little used. This is because it was separated from the National Gallery by four lanes of traffic and from the main body of the square by the drop in level.

To create better connections between the busy lower area to the south, and the empty higher area to the north, it was realised that new, centrally positioned steps were required to facilitate movement between the two. With pedestrianisation of the street in front of the National Gallery and provision of a new grand staircase, centrally positioned to accommodate pedestrian desire lines, the National Gallery is now properly connected to the square, as originally intended. The northern part of the square, with its exceptional views, is now easily accessible to pedestrians gathering at the National Gallery. The improvements also facilitate pedestrian movement along desire lines from Whitehall to the south of the square and to Soho and West End theatres located to the north.

The master plan for the World Squares initiative was produced following eighteen months of extensive public consultation, which included exhibitions and media coverage. Over 80 per cent of people who responded to the consultation exercise were in favour of the proposed changes within the study area.

Improving legibility

Prior to the recent improvements, the axial sight lines and the impressive views out of Trafalgar Square were largely unappreciated. This was because pedestrian movement patterns did not correspond with the sight lines. The areas with the best views were not available to pedestrians because of the vehicular traffic. The site of the square was originally chosen because of its strategic position, where the most important streets and vistas in London converge. The layout had to be amended so that the sight lines and the movement lines could correspond with each other as originally intended.

Prior to the World Squares project, to see the impressive strategic views from within Trafalgar Square required standing in the road or on a tiny traffic island, the King Charles traffic island, off the main part of the square to the south. From this little traffic island existed views along The Mall to Buckingham Palace, along Whitehall to the Houses of Parliament, and along Northumberland Avenue towards the Hungerford Bridge at the River Thames. This traffic island has served as one of the most symbolic spots in London because it contains the oldest structure in Trafalgar Square, a Portland stone plinth and bronze statue of King Charles I, which has been positioned there since 1675. The statue of Charles I faces down Whitehall and directly towards Inigo Jones' Banqueting House, where the king was executed for his unconstitutional behaviour (see Appendix II).

The King Charles statue has now been incorporated into a larger public space off the main square, and although this space still serves as a traffic island to the south of the main square, it is now connected to the main public space and to surrounding streets by surface level pedestrian crossings. The space is now part of the everyday route used by pedestrians and has become a staging post from which people can plan their onwards journeys. From the statue, pedestrians can look directly along the streets they are likely to want to progress down, such as Whitehall, Northumberland Avenue, and The Mall. As a staging post, the area around the statue is appropriate for visitor signage and other facilities, although clearly these need to be carefully designed and sensitively positioned to ensure they do not prejudice the setting of the statue.

The King Charles statue visually directs the pedestrian onwards to greater sights. The unfolding of a series of views in this way reflects what Gordon Cullen[42] referred to as 'serial vision', and what L'Enfant, the master planner of Washington DC, refers to as 'reciprocity of sight'.[43] This approach was developed by the Italian master, Brunelleschi, who arguably started the architectural Renaissance in 1420 after constructing the dome of the cathedral of Santa Maria del Fiore in Florence.

Brunelleschi's work in Florence demonstrates how creating a progression of views within the built environment promotes legibility. It is worth examining how he developed this in Florence in order to appreciate how the same principles apply around Trafalgar Square.

When Brunelleschi had completed the famous dome of Florence Cathedral, he embarked upon reviving the classical concept of relating streets to squares. He did this by connecting two squares with a new street. One of the squares already existed, it was the main cathedral square, but the second square was new. Brunelleschi designed the new square, the Piazza Della Santissima Annunziata,

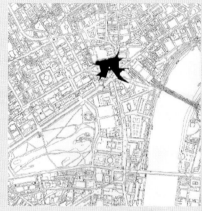

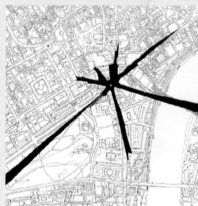

Top. Bill Hillier's 'space syntax' drawing showing the strategic views from the centre of Trafalgar Square. (Courtesy of Professor Bill Hillier/Space Syntax Limited.)

Above. The strategic views from the King Charles traffic island. (Courtesy of Professor Bill Hillier/Space Syntax Limited.)

A SHORT WALK THROUGH FLORENCE

This concept of serial vision is demonstrated on a short walk from the Piazza San Marco, a square that is associated with the University of Florence and is located approximately 100 m to the west of Brunelleschi's Piazza Della Santissima Annunziata. From the Piazza San Marco, the colonnades around the Piazza Della Santissima Annunziata can just be seen down the interconnecting street, as a kind of beckoning landmark (view 1). On walking down the interconnected street towards Brunelleschi's colonnades, the Piazza Della Santissima Annunziata gradually unfolds before one's eyes (view 2). First, more of the colonnades can be seen, and then the enclosing buildings, and then an equestrian statue is revealed standing within the square. This statue serves as a focal point, it is aligned to the south, where it directs the eye down the street that Brunelleschi orientated to connect with the cathedral. Following the statue's orientation, one faces down Brunelleschi's street and sees the major landmark of the cathedral dome (view 3). The whole sequence results in a legible and memorable environment as the pedestrian is pulled onwards to greater sights.

Below. Plan of a sequential route from the Piazza San Marco to the cathedral of Santa Maria del Fiore in Florence.

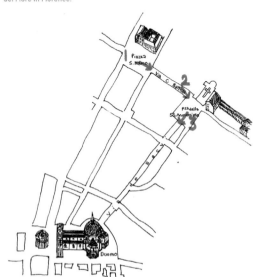

Top Right. View 1: Looking east out of the Piazza San Marco towards the colonnades, around Brunelleschi's Piazza Della Santissima Annunziata...

Middle Right. View 2: As soon as this corner is turned, the Piazza Della Santissima Annunziata is entered and an equestrian statue directs the eye onwards...

Bottom Right. View 3: The equestrian statue directs the eye to the landmark dome upon Florence's cathedral.

Far Left. View from the King Charles traffic island looking down Whitehall to Parliament.

Left. View from the King Charles traffic island looking through Admiralty Arch and down The Mall towards Buckingham Palace.

as a classical composition around the church of the Servite monks who served at the cathedral. This new piece of urban design became part of a Florentine tradition that provides the pedestrian with an unfolding visual experience as they progress through interconnected streets and squares.

Similarly, in Trafalgar Square the statue of Charles I leads the eye to the Banqueting House, and down Whitehall to Parliament, and to the clock tower of Big Ben. The new master plan for Trafalgar Square realised that the King Charles traffic island affords strategic views of some of London's most important vistas, and proposed that it should be better related to the main public space and surrounding streets. This was required to ensure that the square realises its visual potential. The subsequent improvement works increased visual accessibility and legibility by connecting pedestrian movement lines so they correspond with the axial sightlines into and out of the square.

While Norman Foster's proposed master plan did not include pedestrianisation to the southern end of Trafalgar Square, the pedestrian areas were increased in size at the expense of road space. This provided pedestrians with greater priority – crossing points are now shorter, safer, and easier to use.

Bill Hillier identified the proposals within the master plan as being the minimum necessary to create a World Square. Trafalgar Square is now properly integrated with the movement patterns and urban design of the surrounding city. Trafalgar Square will continue to act as state space and to attract large numbers

Right. Since the improvements have been carried out to Trafalgar Square, the Mayor of London has planned a programme of entertainment events attracting a broad cross section of society to the public space.

of tourists, but its new pedestrian connections and facilities, such as a carefully designed cafe and public toilets, will ensure that it is also used by ordinary Londoners. As well as serving as a symbol of national power it can now also bring people together and strengthen the collective identity of those who live in the city. The Mayor of London has introduced *Summer in the Square*, an entertainment and arts programme lasting for three months within Trafalgar Square. The objective for this is to showcase the vast array of cultural activity to be found in London, the UK, and around the world.

Given the strategic nature of the roads and the massive number of vehicles being driven around Trafalgar Square, design interventions affecting traffic have had to be carefully planned. Altering the traffic flow around Trafalgar Square would have serious repercussions for vehicular movement patterns elsewhere in the city. An investigation was therefore required into the effects of closing the north side of the square to traffic and reducing the widths of roads in other areas. The transport study had to be produced concurrently with the master plan to allay fears of gridlock. The Mayor of London put in place traffic management policies that include provision of an effective public transport alternative to the car – this is partly funded by charging drivers for bringing vehicles into the core area of central London.

The popular support received for the World Squares initiative has helped the Mayor of London to extend the vision for squares from the central area to the whole of London. Through the Mayor's 100 Public Spaces Programme, all 33 London Boroughs should have new public space projects. Trafalgar Square demonstrates how a high profile public space project can be used to model the principles and processes that can then be applied across a large urban region.

PERFORMANCE CHECKS: LOCATION AND MOVEMENT

- Has the urban design strategy unravelled the morphology of the streets and blocks to reveal any pattern or hierarchy of public spaces?
- Are any new connections required to enable better pedestrian movement between the spaces?
- Has the urban design strategy suggested how a more logical arrangement of public spaces could be created? For example, have decisions been made to loose any dysfunctional spaces or to create new spaces where important sight lines and pedestrian flows could correspond with each other?
- Has the urban design strategy indicated where a sequence of squares and interconnected streets might benefit from combined action to improve the environment, especially for waking and cycling?
- Have design measures been considered for improving individual squares, for example through provision of unobtrusive servicing areas, or through provision of direct crossing points that assist people going about their daily routines?
- Are there stimulating visual sequences that encourage pedestrians, in particular, to progress through the study area, along interconnected streets and squares?
- Have public transport stops and interchanges been integrated with public spaces to provide a welcoming sense of arrival?
- Has the urban design strategy been integrated with a transportation strategy to ensure that the effects of new proposals on different modes of transport are carefully considered and planned for?

CHAPTER THREE>

CHAPTER THREE
PHYSICAL FORM AND ROBUSTNESS

It is always wise to be fully knowledgeable about a principle in order to violate it judiciously.

J.B. Goldsteen and C.D Elliot, *Designing America*.[44]

All squares have to relate to their unique context and to a unique set of user demands, and as such it may not be appropriate to apply ideal standards to all situations. However, it can be helpful to identify what has worked well in different places and at different times so this can inform current best practice. This approach can also assist in identifying the issues that need to be addressed in the design of public space and the performance criteria against which proposals can be assessed.

This chapter is concerned with the design of a square as a whole and with the arrangement of its various parts, based on principles of practical use and visual cohesion. It addresses details – for example, the transition from the street to a square, the size and shape of a square, spatial enclosure, and the design of subspaces within a square. It is concerned with making public space flexible so that it can accommodate different uses and satisfy changing demands over time. The chapter therefore focuses upon the practical design considerations that will need to be addressed in developing proposals for new public spaces. To begin with, some of the squares and processional routes that have shaped cities in various ages are briefly highlighted as these demonstrate continuing themes.

SQUARES AND PROCESSIONAL ROUTES

Throughout the history of the city, a recurring theme is a centrally located square that is connected to a principal pathway. This pathway often connected the outside world to the city square through a monumental gateway within the city walls. The pathway leading from the main city gates to the central square is usually the most accessible route in ancient cities, and was often given symbolic significance as a processional route.

An illustration of this theme is the work of the ancient Mesopotamian ruler Nebuchadnezzar II, a monumental town planner in the 6th century BC who added significantly to the scale of Babylon. One of the most striking features developed in Babylon during his reign was the Ishtar Gate, the main gateway within the massive city walls. This gateway provided access to the processional way, which was one of the defining features of the city. The Ishtar gateway was huge and included turreted towers to either side. The main gates were probably made of cedar wood overlaid with panels of bronze or gold. Brilliant blue glazed bricks depicting symbolic animals adorned the structure around the gate (part of the structure can be seen in the Pergamon Museum in Berlin, Germany).

The importance of the processional way to Babylonian culture is reflected in the way that it was lined with walls finished in blue glazed bricks, upon which were depicted animals in bright colours (some of which can be seen in the British Museum in London). Even the foundations of these walls were decorated to a level of 18 m below ground level. Every year major celebrations in national life proceeded along the processional way. The way cut through to Babylon's symbolic heart, where an open square contained a massive ziggurat and temple. The ziggurat was a tall pyramid-like structure, probably eight stories high – an impressive landmark that would have drawn the eye of anyone entering through the city gates. The site of the ziggurat endured as a symbolic place for the Babylonians for thousands of years (see Ref. 45 for an account of town planning of Babylon). When Nebuchadnezzar held the Jewish people captive in Babylon in the 6th century BC, the Jews left behind their own temple, its square, and the city walls of Jerusalem, which were all designed with dimensions that were of great religious significance.

The main square in a city of ancient Greece or Rome was often located at the intersection of the settlement's two main streets. These streets were often primary axes running north–south and east–west on a grid street pattern. Although larger than the ancient Mesopotamian walled cities, these settlements usually contained principal pathways that lead through monumental gateways or triumphal arches and onto the main city square.

Within the ancient city of Athens, the Babylonian concept of a processional route that connects with the main square was further developed. Here, the main processional route was the Panathenaic Way, and this was the most connected route in the city. It performed a similar function to Babylon's ancient processional way, and once every year it contained the most important festival procession. This festival was a major event in the collective civic life of Athens, and the Panathenaic Way was far more than an ancient street: '... it served both as a sacred way and also as the main street in Athens'.[35] This closely interconnected relationship between the main processional route and the design of the main square was developed at a scale that was great enough to help to physically define the settlement, as well as being of symbolic significance.

The grid street layout, as seen in major cities in the USA, was probably developed by the ancient Greek architect and town planner Hippodamus when he began to develop the new Ionian city of Miletus in 479 BC. The old city had been destroyed in a Persian attack in 494 BC. Hippodamus embarked on rebuilding Miletus as a thoroughly modern city to rival Athens. The street layout was based on a gridiron plan system, being straight and crossing at right angles. These

Below Left. A triumphal archway located at the junction of Rome's principal street with the Piazza del Popolo.

Below. Triumphal archway in Marseilles in France.

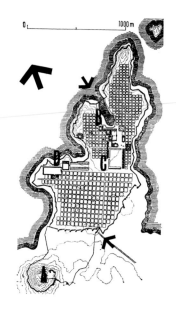

Above. Plan of Miletus in ancient Greece, showing the acropolis (A), the harbour (B), the agora (C), and leisure facilities (D).[11] (Courtesy of Pearson Education Limited.)

streets were of a uniform width and the city blocks between them were also of fairly uniform dimensions. This regular geometric layout created a strong rhythm and a sense of enclosure along the streets, which resulted in the open space of the city square appearing all the more dramatic.

The main city square at Miletus, the agora, was a large centrally located rectangular public space occupying several empty blocks within the street layout. This square was an important business centre and, for practical economic reasons, it was located close to the waterfront for easy access to the port, warehouses, and incoming ships. It was also a place for leisure and had direct access to the theatre, gymnasium, and stadium. Miletus became a prosperous capital and sent out colonists to found 70 urban settlements, always seeking to reproduce the urban conditions of the mother city.

Hippodamus' agora at Miletus included a wall of shops on at least three sides, onto which were attached colonnades, known as 'stoas'. The colonnades at Miletus were one and two stories high, resulting in an interesting mix of enclosed and semi-enclosed space around the square. They protected people from the weather and provided space for shop displays.

The Milesian practice of laying out a whole new town as a single unit, following the gridiron plan system, became commonplace. It provided a simple and equitable method for dividing the land, defined the public and private realms effectively, facilitated an accessible city square, and was effective in defining new districts and neighbourhoods within a settlement. It resulted in a legible environment in which Greek colonists and foreign traders could easily and safely find their way around. A negative factor was that the layout often paid little respect to natural topography or other locally distinctive natural features.

The Milesian plan has subsequently been used all over the world, for both temporary and permanent settlements. More than 2,000 years later, the Milesian grid has been used in cities across the USA, including Portland, Philadelphia, New Haven, and New York. In Manhattan, Fifth Avenue is the most accessible street within the grid layout, and this connects to the lively Washington Square through a triumphal archway. Fifth Avenue functions as a processional route, and the Saint Patrick's Day Parade marches along it, uniting many New Yorkers every year in timeless fashion.

In a similar fashion to the Milesian grid, the 'ideal' cities designed in Europe during the Renaissance period often included streets crossing at right angles, or with other geometric arrangements, with the main square at the centre.

The Renaissance approach to design was also based on the study of perspective and an appreciation of depth in space. New city designs were more focused on the mathematical rules of geometry. Movement through space

Far Left. The triumphant archway at the junction of Fifth Avenue with Washington Square in Manhattan, New York, reflecting ancient urban design principles.

Left. The Saint Patrick's Day Parade along the processional route of Fifth Avenue in Manhattan, New York.

became a preoccupation as powerful members of society wanted to get to places, and quickly. Many rulers of the 17th century were considered to have absolute power by divine right, and in urban design terms this is reflected through an emphasis on the straight line, order, the receding plane, and the long vista, which gave an impression of limitless space. While the new avenues and squares designed by Brunelleschi in the early 15th century and by Michelangelo in the early 16th century were relatively modest interventions within existing historic cities, a much grander scale was to follow. In the 17th century, the views out of squares became almost visually limitless, ending only with follies, such as an obelisk or an arch, or a single building. The closed vista, which had been a feature of many medieval squares, was no longer considered appropriate.

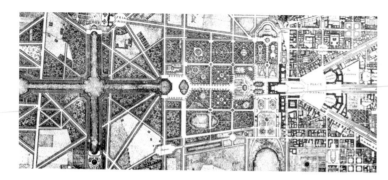

Left. Plan of Versailles, which was designed to be experienced at 15 mph.[11] (Courtesy of Pearson Education Limited.)

Below Left. 'Ideal' Renaissance city plans from 1457 to 1592.[11] (Courtesy of Pearson Education Limited.)

During the late Renaissance period the street and movement along it became the main focuses of a new master planning. The resulting geometric plans appeared to be attractive at a two-dimensional level, when seen on a piece of paper, but they related poorly to the practical physical requirements of the urban population. The plans dictated where uses and institutions should go, but paid little regard to their practical location requirements.

These grand new Renaissance squares often did not perform well as active public spaces. This was because their form followed the function of movement alone, and of visual effect to enhance this movement – they were not accommodating places designed for public gathering, markets, and recreation. Due to the scale of these projects, the old morphology of streets, blocks, and active public spaces, was often swept away. The Renaissance established principles for city design, especially for the monumental route and for the city square, that were to model the heart of growing cities across the world for the next three centuries. The Industrial Revolution and growth of European empires strengthened many capitalist economies, and facilitated implementation of large-scale development projects.

The influence of Renaissance town planning has been far-reaching. When the young nation of the United States of America required a new capital city, the French architect and engineer Pierre Charles L'Enfant combined principles from the Milesian grid with grander notions reflecting the layout of European cities. When he offered his services to President George Washington, L'Enfant claimed that the design of the new city should reflect 'the greatness of the empire'. When the American congress agreed to appoint L'Enfant in 1709 as architect, he borrowed maps of Paris, Amsterdam, Karlsruhe, Turin, and other European cities to assist him with his plans.

A surviving memorandum of L'Enfant's, in which he comments on his own

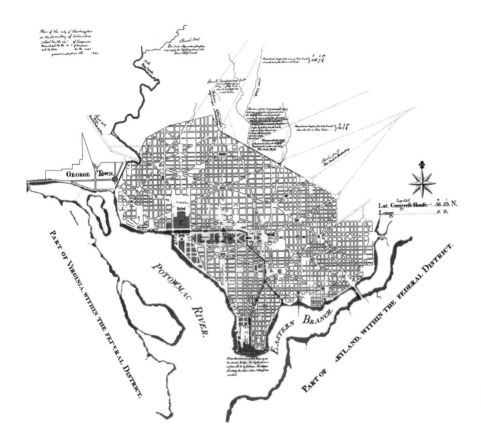

Left. The plan for the capital of the USA
produced by L'Enfant c.1800 – a plan that still
works for Washington DC today. (Produced by
the USA geological survey from the original.)[43]
(Courtesy of the USA Library of Congress.)

proposals for the USA's new capital city, states that he 'made the distribution regular with streets at right angles north–south and east–west.' Over this basic plan form he opened dramatic diagonal avenues from the principal points within the city, such as the Capitol, the president's house, and Lincoln Park. These diagonals were to 'connect each part of the city with more efficacy by...making the real distance less'. Twenty-four open squares and circles were included in L'Enfant's master plan, to mark the intersection of thoroughfares and to function as the focal points for new neighbourhoods. L'Enfant claimed that 'Each square would be within view of the next permitting a reciprocity of sight'.[43]

Although clearly defined axial routes were included in ancient cities (and remain in planned cities, such as Washington DC), unscrambling the most connected sites within the street network of many modern cities can be more difficult. However, as explained in the previous chapter, identifying such accessible sites is a prerequisite to finding an appropriate location for a new city square. (For further information on the historic development of streets and squares see *Town and Square* by Paul Zucker,[10] *City Planning According to Artistic Principles* by Camillo Sitte,[46] *Design of Cities* by Edmund Bacon,[35] and *The City in History* by Lewis Mumford.[9])

TRANSITION FROM STREET TO SQUARE

Squares that can be easily seen from the street by passers-by are clearly more likely to be used than those that are visually obscured. While a square needs to be perceived as being a distinct place, it also needs to be visible and easily accessible to those on the street if it is to be well used. The more that people in the street feel that the square is an extension of the space they are in, the more likely they are to feel invited to enter. An extension of the activity and the design elements found within the square into the connecting streets can help to facilitate this.

On entering the square, the immediate impression should be one of arrival, with a view of an animated scene. The most dominant elements in the view are likely to be noticed first, and the design should help to ensure that attention is drawn to the most important buildings, such as those containing public uses. Building height, scale, density, materials, and colour can all be used to emphasise

Below. These grand pillars create an open visual gateway into Catalunya, a square that terminates Barcelona's processional route of La Rambla.

Below Right. On entering a square from the street there should be an immediate sense of arrival, as shown here in Victoria Square in Birmingham.

the most important buildings and uses around a square. Sunny areas and bright colours are spotted before dull areas, and the position of the sun will have a crucial effect upon how spaces are perceived at different times of the day.

Major changes of level between the street and a square can have a harmful effect upon the use of public space. If a square is either significantly higher or lower than the connecting streets it runs the risk of appearing detached from street activity. Such a change of level can act as a barrier, which will reduce the number of people and amount of activity within a square. Research in Manhattan has shown that public spaces with below average use generally have significant differences in height, architectural barriers, or an absence of seating.[47] As explained in the previous chapter, the street contains the people that are the lifeblood of the square and it is crucial to keep direct visual contact between the pedestrian flows along connecting streets and with people in the square.

When pavements or sidewalks are very busy with high pedestrian flows, as they often are in major cities, it can be an advantage to slightly raise the square, to provide some relief from the human traffic. Partly raised squares can still be successful if they manage to retain visual contact with pedestrian flows on connecting streets and if they have clearly defined entry points into the square. It can feel satisfying to get above the noise and pollution of the street, but if steps have to be climbed to access the square, there must be something at the top of the steps to make the effort worthwhile and to keep people there.

Above. If a space is screened from pedestrian flows, the lack of surveillance attracts antisocial behaviour, as shown here in Hunter Square in Edinburgh.

Left. Steps leading up to Marseilles railway station in southern France, and ...

Below. the view from the top of the steps.

A drop in the level from the street to the square can reduce natural surveillance if the people in the square are below the eye level of people on the street. This has occurred in many of the public squares developed in the post-war period. An eye-catching feature may draw people into a sunken area – but the further down it is, the greater the attraction will have to be, and the more likely it is to become an area with a crime problem due to a lack of natural surveillance.

Consideration should also be given to existing or potential views inbetween streets and squares, and to how views will be protected and enhanced. The characteristics of a view can change throughout the day and the seasons, and so their special qualities must be fully understood and recorded to ensure that future development projects do not have a negative impact on them.

Above. Copley Square in Boston in the USA is similar to many post-war municipal public spaces, and includes sunken areas that attract litter and antisocial activities.

Below. Well-used public space at the new city hall in Toronto, Canada.

SIZE AND SHAPE

The ancient Roman architect Vitruvius Pollio stated that the width of a square should be two-thirds that of its length, because this results in a robust and versatile shape for accommodating both an audience and the spectacles they come to watch. This clearly results in a rectangular plan form. He states:[9]

> The dimensions of the Forum ought to be adjusted to the audience, lest the space be cramped for use, or else, owing to such scanty audience, the Forum should seem too large. Now let the breadth be so determined that when the length is divided into three parts, two are assigned to the breadth. For so the plan will be oblong, and the arrangement will be adapted to the purpose of spectacles.

Vitruvius was concerned about the visual qualities of the Roman forum, and also about its robustness for practical use. He realised that it was essential to understand the users' requirements and that these should inform the design process. The ideas of Vitruvius have been far-reaching and they have had a significant influence on other civilisations. Many of the settlements in the southern and western USA were modelled by the Spanish in accordance with their design code, the *Laws of the Indies*. This code was produced in 1573 under the direction of the Spanish king, Philip the Second, to plan their new towns in the Americas. The laws were based on the classical treatise of Vitruvius Pollio, which

Right. A Catalan square in Spain with robust dimensions, measuring approximately 70 m by 50 m.

the Spanish had studied when developing their military towns ('bastides') when fighting the Moors. A surviving example of a Spanish bastide town is Sante Fe near Granada, founded in 1492.[48]

Ordinance 113 of the *Laws of the Indies* states that the size of the city square should be proportional to the number of inhabitants, and should take into consideration the growth of the town. They planned for the future, hoping that a town's growth would justify the size of its square.[6] The Spanish towns in the Indies were each centred on a main square, which served much like the Roman forum. The square acted as marketplace, meeting place, and as an arena for fiestas, including bull fighting and other tournaments. It was typically surrounded by an arcaded street containing the town's main buildings, such as the church, town hall, and shops. Today, this kind of square survives in Californian cities such as Santa Fe.

The *Laws of the Indies* Ordinance 112 stated that, for a square, a rectangular shape was best for accommodating fiestas, especially if horses were being used, and a minimum size was set for the main square of 162 m by 244 m – which would have resulted in an enormous open space. Kevin Lynch recommends that the limit for either the length or width of a square should be 25 m if it is to result in a pleasant human scale.[48] This reflects the maximum distance at which people are able to see other people's facial expressions. Carr *et al.* closely support Lynch's figures, and state that the most successful spaces are under 22 m in length or width.[49] This is a reflection of the more intimately enclosed squares found in European medieval towns. However, Gehl considers that larger maximum dimensions can be considered, between 70 m and 100 m, as this is the maximum distance for being able to see the events that people are engaged in.[50]

Camillo Sitte advised that the average dimensions for the squares in ancient cities are approximately 140 m by 60 m. However, he also states that exact rules in this matter are of little worth because the actual effect will depend largely on the position of the observer. Notwithstanding this, he states that there are few city squares that are actually square in shape, and that those few are unattractive as he favours a more irregular and organic layout. He also claims that squares with a length that is more than three times the breadth 'have a scarcely better appearance'.[46] Cultural and climatic factors are also acknowledged as being important considerations in determining a square's form.

There will often be practical and aesthetic reasons for why the shape of the square should be irregular – for example, to open an important view – and such squares can retain a formal dignity as long as they retain an appropriate sense of enclosure. Camillo Sitte claimed that: [46]

> When we begin to examine ... past epochs we see that irregular squares can be more readily adorned with statues and monuments for they do not lack suitable places for them.

When considering the shape of a new square, and the arrangement of the buildings that will enclose it, it is helpful to remember that, in practice, the eye will often not appreciate what appears to be perfect on the plan. Therefore, caution is required when following any rigidly symmetrical plans. Sitte advised that: [46]

> Whoever studies a map of his own city can be convinced that violent irregularities shown on the map, do not in the least seem to be striking irregularities when seen on the ground.

Even fairly major irregularities in the shapes of squares are usually only seen in plan form. Such irregularities can help to conceal the gaps caused by the streets that enter the square, which could otherwise harm the sense of enclosure. (See Rob Krier's *Urban Space* for a morphological study of the shapes of squares.[51])

It may be difficult to justify developing a city square with dimensions large enough to accommodate special events that occur only occasionally, especially as large areas of the square are then underused at other times, but well-designed subspaces within the main square can go some way to remedying this. (The design of subspaces will be discussed in greater detail later in this chapter.) Some events may only occur once or twice a year, but they may be important for the collective identity of the urban community and it is therefore essential that spaces exist to accommodate them. Other events, such as a market, may occur more frequently, and when such uses have finished, the space allocated to them should be cleared so that space is available for other activities.

As we have already seen, large city squares, such as London's Trafalgar Square, serve a necessary role in democratic life, not least because they can accommodate large gatherings of people. However, we have also seen that prior to the World Squares project Trafalgar Square did not function in a way that encourages the kind of daily human interaction that is associated with so many historic European squares. If a square is to realise its potential as a focal point for human activity, it is crucial that there are sufficient people to animate its space.

While ancient civilizations could sometimes build squares large enough to accommodate the whole urban population, today this is impossible unless large tracts of the city are cleared to create spaces such as Beijing's Tiananmen Square, which is so vast that any sense of urban place is lost. The size and shape of the square should reflect its likely use and relate to the numbers of people that are likely to use it. If a consensus can be drawn from the opinions of the other commentators mentioned it is that a rectangular shape is most robust for a range of activities and events, and for practical and aesthetic effect the width to length ratio should normally be between 1:2 and 1:3. As a rough guide, a public space measuring 50 m by 70 m can usually accommodate most of the uses associated with city squares, and will be of a size that enables an individual to see and comprehend the total space and the activity within it. The performance of a square can be evaluated in terms of how well its shape and size is fit for its purpose – for example, most city squares will be expected to accommodate adults and children who are walking, sitting, watching, eating, trading, meeting, and playing.

SPATIAL ENCLOSURE AND VISUAL COHESION
Successful city squares are defined by coherent architectural compositions that result in a pleasant sense of enclosure.

These qualities are dependent upon the length and width of a square, and upon the scale, height, and proportions of surrounding buildings and other architectural features. Prior to the Renaissance period, squares could be much smaller than they often need to be today to make a visual impact. This is because streets were narrower and carried much less traffic, and so a smaller open space was sufficient to contrast with them.

Sense of enclosure
The German architect Hermann Maertens calculated that a person's range of clear vision is at an angle of about 27 degrees. This translates to a ratio of 1:2. So, to

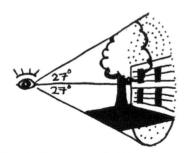

Above. A building's elevation will fill the upper half of an observer's 'cone of vision' if the observer's distance from the building is no greater than twice its height. The lower half of the cone is taken up by the ground surface.[6]

Below. A satisfying sense of enclosure within the Piazza Navona in Rome, with a width to height ratio of approximately 1:2 (excluding the height of the dome and towers of the church).

view a building clearly and easily, the viewer needs to stand away from the building, at a distance that is twice the building's height. If the viewer stands away from the building at a distance that is three times greater than the building is high, at a ratio of 1:3 (18 degrees), the viewer will get a sharper view of the building against its surroundings, and at 1:4 (12 degrees), the observer will see the building as part of the wider townscape and can appreciate its contribution to the skyline – although the sense of enclosure will be weak at this distance (see S. Kostof, *The City Assembled*[6]).

To create a balanced sense of enclosure, the buildings around a city square need to be seen close to, without being so close that they excessively dominate the square or create too strong a sense of enclosure (which may result in a sense of claustrophobia). Conversely, the surrounding buildings should not appear too far away – as if they are floating in the distance – which is the kind of experience provided by the vast communist squares, such as Tiananmen Square in Beijing in China.

When the whole elevation of surrounding buildings can be seen from within the square, their individual architectural designs can be appreciated, along with the way they interrelate to form a townscape composition around the square. To be able to view this effect, the ratio between the size of the square and the height of the buildings needs to be about 1:2. Camillo Sitte advises that 1:2 should be the maximum ratio between building height and the dimensions of the square – unless the form, purpose, and design of the buildings will support greater dimensions. Furthermore, he considers that neither the length nor width of the square should be less than the height of its principal building. When measuring building heights for this purpose, it is the massing of the building that is important, including the main body of the building and its roof. Lesser structures, such as towers and domes, can usually be disregarded.

When the buildings around a square are four or five stories high (and assuming an average range for floor to ceiling heights and for a pitched roof), a comfortable sense of enclosure results if the dimensions of the open square are between 35 and 75 m. This corresponds to a relationship between building height and the length or width of the square, as a ratio, of between 1:2 and 1:4. These parameters for the dimensions of the open space within a square fall within those recommended by Kevin Lynch. The traditional medieval squares of Europe, favoured by Camillo Sitte, also usually reflect these proportions.

A city square should be a showpiece of the built environment, and as such it is vital that it reflects basic rules of architectural proportion. In assessing how a proposed square is likely to perform, one of the key considerations is the relationship between the size of the square and the height of the surrounding buildings. If the surrounding buildings are too low the sense of enclosure will be weak, and the open area of the square will appear too large – and if the surrounding buildings are too high they will appear excessively dominant, and the square, too small. Achieving an appropriate sense of enclosure is therefore a vital consideration. The Renaissance architect Alberti claimed:[52]

> For my part I would have a square twice long as broad, and the porticoes and other buildings about it should answer in some proportion to the open area in the middle, that it may not seem too large, by means of the lowness of the buildings, nor too small, from their being too high. A proper height for the buildings about a square is one third of the breadth of the open area, or one sixth at the least.

However, such ratios cannot be applied *ad infinitum* – there are limits. If these limits are exceeded there will be no increase in either robustness or visual quality. Camillo Sitte provides a good analogy:[46]

> It has been observed that the intensity of sound produced by a men's choir is increased at once by voices that are added to it, but there is a point at which the maximum effect is reached and at which the addition of more singers ceases to improve it. (This point is reached with 400 singers.)

When there is an existing principal building, around which a new square is to be developed, the scale of the principal building will be a crucial consideration in determining the dimensions of the open space within the square. This was the case for Michelangelo's Piazza del Campidoglio in Rome, where the senatorial palace was the principal building. Michelangelo was a master of applying new architectural principles to existing medieval structures. At the Capitoline Hill in Rome, in 1536, he took an amorphous space defined by an irregular group of three medieval buildings and created the masterpiece of the Piazza del Campidoglio from it. The site was at the heart of Rome and beside the ancient imperial forum.

Composition

The new design order and unity of Michelangelo's Campidoglio in 16th century Rome resulted from his restructuring of three existing medieval buildings into a new symmetrical composition. The senatorial palace, which serves as Rome's town hall, was centrally placed in the group as the principal building. Michelangelo remodelled the frontage of the palace so that its tower, which was previously off-centre, became a centrally positioned focal point. The design axis from the tower sent a force out across the square and into medieval Rome. This axis was to affect the future arrangement of roads and buildings within the growing city. The use of a tower as an axis of a square, around which a new architectural composition would be formed, reflected the approach of the ancient Romans, who made similar use of classical pediments upon principal building elevations.

Michelangelo added small extensions and new classically styled facades onto the three existing buildings at the Piazza del Campidoglio, but the original fabric can still be seen today if the backs of the buildings are inspected. This remodelling of the existing buildings, rather than complete redevelopment, was a sustainable way of saving on resources.

Michelangelo's surface treatment of the public space at the Piazza del Campidoglio also plays a critical role in unifying the design. Bacon claims that:

Below. Michelangelo's remodelled senatorial palace with its centrally positioned tower, within the Piazza del Campidoglio in Rome.

> One of the greatest attributes of the Campidoglio composition is the modulation of the land. Without the shape of the oval, and its two-dimensional star-shaped paving pattern, as well as its three dimensional projection in the subtly designed steps that surround it, the unity and coherence of the design would not be achieved.[35]

This modular approach was effective in creating a coherent and unified design. In applying such a module, a grid is mapped over a plan of the site. This grid facilitates a mathematical relationship in the positioning of all of the design components within the square. It ensures that each design component, including buildings, steps, and statues, can be located with a mathematical relationship with each other, and with the square as a whole. This approach can be as relevant for the design of public space today as it was in the 16th century.

It was during the later Renaissance, especially the period characterised by the Baroque, that the design of statues, fountains, and other ornamental street furniture became important in organising the space within a square, and for relating all components within a square into a formal architectural composition. Renaissance architecture was based on the classical orders, as interpreted from surviving buildings and ancient books – such as those produced by Vitruvius. Ancient Greece and Rome provided the aesthetic of column, entablature, pediment, and architectural detailing, which was established and standardised according to the Tuscan, Doric, Ionic, Corinthian, and Composite orders.

The earlier medieval elevations had often included a random fenestration arrangement, with large areas of solid masonry and occasional small windows for reasons of defence. As a result of more stable and powerful government, architects began to explore more creative relationships between solid mass and the void of space, as promoted by Alberti. They began to arrange structural elements and fenestration patterns to create new rhythms and order, providing richly detailed elevations on the buildings around public squares.

The Piazza San Marco in Venice provides an excellent example. It was much visited by the grand tourists from Northern Europe, especially during the early

Left. The Maison Carrée, a well-preserved Roman temple in Nîmes in France, built over 2,000 years ago. It shows the classical detailing that influenced Renaissance design.

18th century. The Venetian artist Canaletto produced many paintings of Venice for this burgeoning tourist market, and these paintings reflected the Renaissance taste for idealised architectural compositions:[53]

> Canaletto often fuses multiple, and sometimes invented, viewpoints. Some of the views are from angles blocked by buildings that his imagination would simply remove, opening up the scene like a stage set. He alters the proportions and shapes of individual buildings and sometimes includes buildings that are not there.

Below. Canalleto's idealised painting of the Piazza San Marco in Venice, dating from the 1750s. Building proportions are altered to create an ideal composition. (From an oil canvas, courtesy of the National Gallery, London.)

The creation of architectural unity and the imposition of order is one of the key achievements of Renaissance design. This approach takes its cue from classical architecture, but raised it to new heights of elaboration. In the design of the city square, the individual physical elements are subordinated to the identity of the whole composition.

Palladio's architecture was arguably the first to succeed in transferring the two-dimensional relationship of a facade to the whole complex of a three-dimensional composition,[10] but many Renaissance architects were to master the technique. Architectural elements such as colonnades and arcades were to be used to connect the various parts of a square, and to increase the unity of the facades surrounding it. There was to be an increasing appreciation of depth in space along the horizontal and the vertical, and consideration was given to how building facades interconnect with the open squares.

As consideration was given to movement through space, so once again consideration was given to the processional routes entering into city squares. The main pathway was not necessarily a road, for example in Venice it is the Grand Canal, which is

lined with Renaissance palaces. The canal meanders through the city and eventually arrives at the Piazza San Marco, providing a breathtaking sense of arrival.

Renaissance designers such as Michelangelo and Brunelleschi modulated the elevations of buildings that enclosed squares, as well as the open space within the square. They excelled in arranging architectural elements of elevations to create rational and satisfying compositions. Giedion comments that by 1500, '...we find windows ranged upon windows, each treated as a separate feature and accentuated by a pediment, pilasters, or columns, yet rhythmically articulated to one another'.[54]

When buildings are developed on narrow plots of less than 7 m in width, there tends to be a fine urban grain with a vertical emphasis. 'Urban grain' refers to the vertical definition of buildings along a street or square. During the medieval period, it was the width of the footprint of individual buildings that largely determined the urban grain. Medieval plots were narrow because of the high value of land and the multitude of uses that had to be contained within the restrictive city walls. The buildings around early Renaissance squares often included a fine urban grain because of the existing narrow medieval plot widths, but as the Renaissance period progressed and demands for space grew, plot sizes became larger. Architectural designs remained visually coherent and stimulating as architectural elements, such as windows, doors, balconies, and pilasters, became articulated into 'bays'. These bays are architectural compartments, which are usually based on structural divisions. They break up large elevations into a more familiar scale, stimulating urban grain. In modern times, space requirements continue to grow and maintaining the urban grain remains an issue.

Above Left. Wide public elevations need to be articulated into 'bays' to maintain a fine urban grain, as with the Renaissance palaces along the Grand Canal in Venice.

Above Right. A fine urban grain exists in the old town of Nice in France due to its narrow building plots and relatively tall buildings.

If the plot depth of an individual building measures less than 15 m from front to back, this can also promote a robust and environmentally sustainable form of design. This is because at such a depth the building can receive natural light and ventilation both to the front and to the rear, which saves on air conditioning and the use of artificial lights. (See also Chapter Four of *Responsive Environments* by Bentley *et al.*[12])

Consideration also needs to be given to how the buildings around a square are defined along the horizontal plane, and to how they progress from the ground to the sky. Classical buildings are usually arranged to include a base, or 'plinth', which appears relatively strong and solid, even though several stories can be accommodated within it. Above the plinth is the main body of the building, which contains most of the accommodation and the principal stories. Above this is the 'attic' level, where architectural elements appear lighter and are often of a diminished scale. When the buildings around a square reflect these hierarchies, visual cohesion is likely to be strong. The heights and proportions of buildings around city squares often vary significantly and in a random way, but can still result in dynamic architectural compositions. This can be seen in some of the squares and parks of New York, but even here the skyscrapers reflect a hierarchy and progression from the ground to the sky.

Continuous frontages

The streets that access into the square will cause breakages in its frontage. When these streets are more than a few metres wide they can damage the design cohesion and the sense of enclosure. Camillo Sitte states that this problem can be reduced by making streets enter the square from different directions and at different angles, following the form of turbine arms. This arrangement can mean that from any single spot within a square only one access point can be seen and that, apart from this one break, the building frontage will appear to be continuous. This is because all of the other entry points are positioned out of the line of sight. Sitte claims that this reflects the approach used since the Middle Ages by joiners and masons to hide joints in wood and stone.

Including colonnades or arcades around a square can add to its visual cohesion and provide protection from the weather, as demonstrated by the ancient Greek agora and Roman forum. Brunelleschi's Piazza Della Santissima Annunziata in Florence also includes colonnades around the Renaissance square, which help to define the formal architectural composition.

Skyline

In the same way that careful consideration is required for the design of the transition from the street to the square, and from the inside of buildings to the

Below. Plan of the cathedral square at Ravena in Italy. From any part of the square only one street can be seen to break the sense of enclosure.[46]

open square, it must also be given to the transition from the buildings to the sky. The skyline created by the buildings around a square is an important factor in the creation of visual cohesion. Building elements, such as roofs, chimneys, domes, and towers, should create an interesting silhouette that can be seen from within the square and connecting streets. (See Chapter Four of *Public Places – Urban Spaces* by Moughtin, Oc and Tiesdell[8] for analysis on the design of the skyline.)

Corner buildings

When the buildings that stand on the corner of the access points into a square are designed in an architecturally distinctive way, the access points remain clearly defined. Another way of reducing the impact of access points on the sense of enclosure within a square is to include an architectural portal over a street where it enters into the square. This results in a bridge effect, enabling traffic to access the square while continuing the architectural frontage around the square and providing accommodation above the entry point. A portal bridge can promote a sense of enclosure within the square and can help to screen unsightly views from within it, but there is a risk that it could reduce legibility of the view into the square from the surrounding streets and thereby reduce its visibility to potential users. One way around this problem is to design the portal as a landmark feature in itself. In this way it can have a positive effect upon legibility and perform a similar design function to the Roman triumphal arch, encouraging people to pass under it and to enter the square.

Corner buildings around a square are particularly important as they usually stand at the meeting of at least two visual planes and are at the junction of pedestrian flows. They define the access points into the square and play a key role in creating a sense of

Left. The best Manhattan skyscrapers are articulated into three distinctive sections, including a solid base, a main stem, and tapered top which meets the sky.

Below. Dramatic chimneys designed by Antoni Gaudí punctuate the Barcelona skyline. (Palau Güell, 1886–90, Barcelona, Spain.)

enclosure and visual composition. Due to their prominence they provide the best opportunity for embellishment, and it is essential that they include the majority of public and active uses, such as cafes and bars where people are likely to meet.

Corner buildings should help to create a sense of interest and incident within the street scene. When they include large windows that reveal the activity within public buildings, they create a display that is more effective than any advertisement. (See Chapter Three of *Public Places – Urban Spaces* by Moughtin, Oc and Tiesdell[8] for a comprehensive analysis of different typologies of corner buildings.)

Principal buildings

The Italian tradition of positioning principal buildings within a square is to avoid central or free-standing locations – this applies equally to churches. These principal buildings are often attached to other buildings, and are positioned to the sides of the square. Camillo Sitte observed that of the 255 churches standing in Rome in the late 19th century, 206 had two or three sides attached to neighbouring buildings and 41 had one side attached. When only one or two sides

Below Far Left. Projecting windows on a corner building in Barcelona provide a sense of surveillance over the public realm.

Below Left. A popular Manhattan meeting point, located at the convergence of pedestrian flows and visual planes.

Below Right. Corner detailing on a London building, which provides good views for residents and surveillance over the public realm.

Below Far Right. Celebrating the corner in Toronto.

of the principal building are presented onto the square, resources can then be concentrated on making these public elevations very impressive. Unsightly maintenance areas, yards, and service bays are kept away from public view.

When a principal building within a square is set back or forward from the prevailing building lines, is positioned to the side of the open space, and attached to other buildings, it tends to have a natural relationship with the surrounding townscape and can help to articulate subspaces within the square. It also affords more interesting views of the principal building from a variety of angles.

PUBLIC BUILDINGS

Buildings can help to generate activity and pedestrian flows when they contain popular public uses, such as a town hall, cathedral, or library. When these buildings are designed with clear entrances and include large windows that reveal people inside, they generate a sense of life and activity and provide valuable surveillance over the public realm. Public buildings can be effective anchors, which draw crowds of people to parts of the square that might otherwise be empty. According to the Library Association in the UK, in 1997/98, 356 million visits were made to public libraries (compared with 26 million visits to football matches) – 58 per cent of the UK population hold library cards.

It is particularly appropriate for a city's central library to be located within a city square. A library provides an alternative public seat of learning, where people from all walks of life can enjoy a civilised public environment. The philanthropist Andrew Carnegie, who was born a working class Scot in 1835 and became a famous US steel magnate, built 2,800 libraries across the English-speaking world. He claimed 'There is no such a cradle of democracy upon the earth as the free public library, this republic of letters where neither rank, office, nor wealth receives the slightest consideration'.

The grandeur of 19th and early 20th century libraries, and their prominent locations within city squares, often beside city halls, demonstrates the importance placed on learning. The library was recognised as being an integral part of the civic identity of a city. It is only from the latter half of the 20th century onwards that the status of public libraries seems to have diminished.

The recent resurgence of urban design, and the raising of the status of the public realm, is now also helping to raise the status of public buildings. As new city squares are being created, so are new or improved public buildings being developed around them, including public libraries. These libraries can play an important part in re-educating people in the importance of the public realm and how to value public services. Public spaces and buildings can provide the

Below. The splendid New York Central Library, within the public space of Bryant Park in Manhattan.

resources and environment for individuals and communities to improve themselves. The City of Toronto in Canada provides an example – the council's development of Dundas Square on the main Yonge Street is to enhance the city's world image and provide an improved public presence for the University at Victoria and Dundas.

In Peckham, south London, Southwark Council has developed a new town square with a dramatic new public library and leisure centre. The entrance to the library is through a spacious lobby, which opens directly off the square. Within the lobby is a one-stop-shop dealing with all sorts of local queries. Above the lobby is a multimedia centre that provides adult learning, computer training, and access to the internet. All of these activities create a sense of activity, which spills out into the square and adds to its vitality. Modern construction techniques allow for large voids within curtain walls, which can facilitate a greater visual connection between the interior of buildings and the public realm – this is especially important for public buildings around city squares.

While public buildings are especially important, commercial retail uses also have a clear role to play in city squares. They need to be located along the ground-floor frontages, beside pedestrian flows where they will generate activity and add visual interest.

RESIDENT COMMUNITIES

If security guards or closed-circuit television are required within a square, other than during major events, something has gone wrong and the activity generated within it is insufficient to provide adequate natural surveillance. In such cases, a greater mix of land uses could be considered, or possibly increased building density and intensity of uses around the square.

One of the most effective ways of ensuring that a city square has activity and natural surveillance throughout the day and evening is through establishing a resident community within the surrounding buildings. When people live around a square they are likely to develop a caring sense of ownership for it as they will have a stake in its well-being. People who spend part of their working day in the square, or who only occasionally visit, are less likely to share the commitment to the upkeep of a square than would a settled residential community.

The residential areas around a square are historically located in the stories above ground-floor level, where floor space is cheaper and quieter. Provision of large windows, balconies, and terraces will enable residents to see and enjoy life within the square, while they themselves provide a sense of activity and valuable surveillance. As residents watch over the public realm, the square becomes self-

Above. The award winning new Peckham library in south London.

Top Right. The undistinguished old library building in Peckham.

Above Right. The new Peckham library stands beside a new leisure centre, all within a new urban square.

Right. Peckam's new square and public buildings are helping to regenerate deprived neighbourhoods in the surrounding areas of south London.

policing – this is especially important later in the evening when the businesses on the ground floor have closed and workers have gone home.

When residents collectively control the management of their building they are more likely to become committed long-term residents, which can add to the stability of an area. The inclusion of a mixture of apartment sizes and tenures around a square will help to create a social balance, and will better accommodate the needs of different individuals and families within the housing market.

The normal planning requirements for standards of car parking can be relaxed if public transport is readily available to a square's resident and working populations. Reducing the parking provision helps to reduce traffic pollution, and encourages people to walk, increasing activity and the self-policing of the public realm.

Internal planning

To make effective use of the space within the buildings around a square, the space allocated for services and for circulation, including corridors and stairs, needs to be kept to a minimum. Internal circulation space can be reduced when several different units within a building are accessed from communal lobbies and stairwells. These communal areas are usually accessed from entrance doorways that are regularly spaced around the square. Providing communal entrances to the upper floors also helps to rationalise the number of residential doorways onto the square and provides an easily controlled entry point for effective security. As Alberti explains:[52]

> Vestibules, halls, and other places of public reception in houses ought to be like squares and other open places in cities, not in a remote private corner, but in the centre and most public place ... moreover, the house should not have above one entrance, to the intent that nobody may come in nor anything be carried out, without the knowledge of the porter.

These entry points are often interesting design features in themselves, but they need to be reasonably narrow to leave as much space as possible for commercial uses, which generate more activity.

Successful residential apartments above ground-floor level usually have access from a communal circulation space that has a street-level entrance. They seldom have their primary entrance from within ground-floor units. Research has shown that in the majority of cases where there is not a separate outside access to the upper stories, the space in these areas is left empty, underused, or in a poor condition.[55] Not making effective use of the upper stories is an environmentally unsustainable waste of resources as it increases pressure to develop new land.

The communal stairwells that provide access to units above ground-floor level are often designed as service zones, containing all essential facilities, such as lifts, storage areas, service pipes, emergency exits, and roof access hatches. In effect, the service zones are 'hard' areas, which remain fixed, while the spaces inbetween them are 'soft' and can be adapted to suit the requirements of different occupants over time. This is a robust and sustainable way to build. It provides for a degree of flexibility that helps to ensure that effective use can always be made of the building. This flexibility maximises the return from the initial investment of money and natural resources that went into the building. (See *Responsive Environments* by Bentley *et al.*,[12] page 65.) Intelligent interior planning should result in bathrooms and kitchens being located in close proximity to each other throughout a building. This will reduce the investment required in plumbing and other services, and helps to avoid unsightly drainage pipes traversing building elevations.

VISUAL RICHNESS AND HUMAN SCALE

The human body is an instinctive standard of comparison when considering the size of something. If people can physically relate to different parts of a square through the scale of their own bodies, they are likely to find the space easy to comprehend. While buildings and other defining features need to relate to the scale of the square as a whole to result in a coherent composition, other features can be articulated in a way that reflects a human scale.

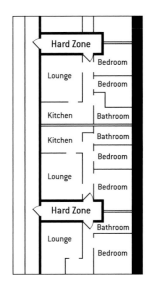

Above. A robust and sustainable building form results from regularly spaced 'hard zones', which are designed to contain all required building services, leaving flexible space inbetween that can be adapted to changing needs.

Left. When design features such as public art reflect a human scale, people are encouraged to interact with them, as shown here in Victoria Square in Birmingham.

Above. Visual richness provided by a decorative shopfront in Barcelona.

Left. Architectural embellishment on a Manhattan corner building.

The square and its enclosing buildings will be many times larger than a human figure, but it is the way that space and building elevations are arranged and detailed that can reflect a human scale. For example, by regularly spacing and grouping design elements across a large surface area, the surface can appear to have more familiar and comprehensible dimensions. Three-dimensional features also have a crucial role to play in defining space, as will be discussed in the section on public art.

While human activity is of prime importance, the way that people perceive the city square will also be influenced by the visual richness that it offers. Visual richness depends on the number of design elements that are on view, and how they relate to each other. If the number of design elements visible on a structure number between five and nine, it will probably provide enough visual interest to appear stimulating.[12] Within a city square, the design elements seen in any one view could include architectural features such as windows or balconies.

When such elements are arranged in a composition that exceeds the upper limit of nine elements, the design can become overly repetitive and may be perceived as being less stimulating because there are too many design elements. In effect, they begin to appear as one superelement rather than individual elements that interrelate with each other. Conversely, when there are fewer than five elements within a design composition, there is a risk of a bland appearance.

The effectiveness of this approach will be influenced by viewing angles, viewing distances, and the orientation of surfaces – a subject that was thoroughly investigated by John Ruskin on his visits to Venice. The main viewing areas within a city square will be from the pedestrian flows, and especially from well-used seating areas beside these flows. Visual richness is therefore best applied to the areas that can be seen from these locations (see *Responsive Environments* by Bentley *et al.*,[12] pages 89–98). The intensity of detail and architectural decoration should be finest in those areas that are closest to potential viewers. The further away the viewers are, the less fine the detailing needs to be, although shapes and forms become more important with increased distance.

DESIGNING SUBSPACES

A city square will usually have to accommodate different types of activity at different times. For instance, some people may want to move quickly and directly across the square and so look for clear spaces that provide routes across it, while others may want to sit next to pedestrian flows so they can watch the world go by, and others may seek a quiet space away from the hustle and bustle. Therefore, the design of the square should provide some articulation of the open space to accommodate different users. The creation of subspaces can be achieved through selective changes in levels or through the arrangement of buildings, planting, seating, or art works. This kind of subdivision also helps to make the city square look fuller when there are few people about, which can be essential for very large spaces.

Creating subspaces can help to create a visually stimulating city square, and will offer greater opportunity for people to find the kind of space that they are looking for.

The vertical depth resulting from a change of level can often appear to be interesting, especially if the upper level provides an elevated viewing place, ideal for people watching and for feeling above it all. The steps between levels can act as ready-made seats, and wider decks can be used as a stage for entertainers, although, as previously mentioned, care is required not to visually segregate the

Above. The steps and water feature in Victoria Square in Birmingham are aligned with the classical town hall, and link two of the square's subspaces in a dramatic way.

Left. Steps combined with a water feature make an interesting link between two subspaces. This feature in Barcelona also provides vertical depth and numerous places to sit and interact with the water.

square from the pedestrian flows that feed into it. It is important also to remember that all areas of the square require natural surveillance to provide a form of self-policing to reduce the chances of criminal activity occurring.

To support the visual cohesion and identity of the square as a whole, the design needs to provide clear connections from subspaces to the main body of the square, and to pedestrian flows that are essential for a feeling of security. Subspaces should be designed to be open, affable, and beckoning,[65] so they remain clearly public rather than private enclaves. If the demarcation of subspaces is subtle, people are unlikely to feel that they have been segregated from activity, or may feel that they are invading another's personal space. Equally, subspaces should not be so large that people feel intimidated by the sense of exposure. Ground treatment, building lines, public art, and landscaping can all help to define subspaces while also unifying them with the whole square. These features can also be used to define areas of movement and areas of rest.

The concept of design modules is an architectural tool that is most likely to be used when a square involves a lot of hard surface construction, rather than earth shaping and informal planting. As explained earlier in this chapter, the modular approach allows different components of the overall design to be interrelated with each other by mapping a grid over the base map of the site. Design modules can help to coordinate materials, shapes, and patterns. They ensure that each part of the design is accurately connected to the whole. However, the design and construction of a square will not be as rigid as with a building, and too much regularity may appear too formal and inflexible. While modules can be a useful tool, care is required to ensure that the result is not unduly regimented.

In Birmingham in the UK the urban design strategy for the city centre resulted in a redesign of Victoria Square, which stands in front of the town hall and the Council House. The revamped square was opened in 1993 and has proved to be a great success. This success partly derives from its detailing and art works, which encourage people to physically interact with them – for example, many surfaces are designed for sitting on. There is a gradient rise of approximately 5 m from the south to the north of Victoria Square, and the design exploits this topography by creating two main subspaces. Grand stone steps and a cascading water feature add a vertical dimension to the square, and these features are of a scale that relate to the surrounding classically inspired buildings. Along the steps and water feature there are both human movement and rest, all under the watchful eye of a female statue, which rests in a pool at the head of the cascading water (locally known as the 'floozie in the jacuzzi'!). The steps and cascading water link two robust subspaces, each measuring approximately 50 m by 30 m. Each subspace has the dimensions of a medium-sized square and they are both used for many activities and civic events.

CREATING A PLEASANT MICROCLIMATE

It can be useful to know something about how climatic factors influence the microclimate to ensure that pleasant conditions exist within a city square. The city square needs to be designed to meet its users' demands at different times of the day and night, and throughout the seasons of the year. To do this, the atmospheric conditions that affect the square and its surroundings need to be understood, including how the sunlight and areas of shadow change, and what the rainfall pattern and temperature range are likely to be. The way that the climate influences urban design is a major subject in itself, and so is only touched upon in this study. (For more information see *Design with Climate* by Victor Olgyay.[56])

Any local peculiarities or outstanding characteristics of the climate within a study area need to be recorded within the contextual analysis produced as part of an urban design strategy. Local people and city authorities should be able to provide some details about local conditions, and the records of the regional meteorological office can also be useful. Site conditions need to be thoroughly understood because the topography and drainage conditions of the site and its surroundings will affect the landscaping design and microclimate within a city square.

A city square's microclimate will be the result of the movement and mixing of heat, water vapour, airborne impurities, light, and sound. This cocktail of natural elements, pollutants, and energy, is influenced by the different surfaces and obstacles that it encounters. A crucial factor influencing the microclimate is the heat level that results from an interchange between the sun and the earth, and this can change markedly through the day and the seasons. The choice of materials within a city square will therefore have a significant effect upon its microclimate.

Sunlight and ventilation

As the sun's energy passes through the earth's atmosphere, it loses more strength the further it has to travel. This means that sites located at latitudes away from the equator will receive less of the sun's energy than those closer to the equator. About one-third of the sun's energy is reflected back into space, especially by the surface of clouds, while the rest is absorbed, heating the land, oceans, and atmosphere. The heated earth radiates infrared energy back into space, but on the way some of it is absorbed and retained by gases in the atmosphere, especially carbon dioxide. Large quantities of carbon dioxide are released by the burning of fossil fuels, and due to the activities of humans there is too much of it to be used up by the earth's forests and oceans. As a result, carbon dioxide accumulates in the earth's atmosphere, along with other 'greenhouse gases', preventing some of the radiated heat from the earth escaping back into space. These gases perform a similar function to the glass in a greenhouse – they let heat in but prevent it from escaping. This process is believed to be resulting in global warming.

To reduce global warming, consumption of fossil fuels needs to be reduced, and effective alternative sources of energy need to be explored. Buildings and public spaces can be designed for 'passive solar gain', whereby they make use of the energy directly available from the sun in the form of solar heat, daylight, and wind. Buildings and spaces designed for passive solar gain are likely to require less heating, lighting, ventilation, and cooling by artificial means, and thereby reduce the demands for energy.

Urban designers, architects, and planners all have roles to play in tackling global warming through the design of the built environment. Developing new or improved public spaces and buildings provides a high-profile opportunity to implement passive solar gain techniques, which can then be explained to users and visitors (*Planning for Passive Solar Design*[57] by Terence O'Rourke plc is a useful guide for planners).

Consideration needs to be given to the way that squares, and the spaces within surrounding buildings, are oriented to the sun and prevailing winds. The ancient Roman architect Vitruvius went to considerable lengths to ensure that space was designed to interact with climatic conditions in a way that supported its intended use and maximised the comfort of its occupants. His approach remains valid today.

When buildings around a city square are designed for passive solar interaction, they are likely to include features such as glazed walls, clerestory windows, and, if there is a deep plan form, atriums. Large areas of glass oriented to the sun require external blinds or louvres to prevent interiors from overheating on bright sunny days. These elements can be designed as architectural features in their own right, rather than being extraneous additions.

When a square and the buildings around it have been designed to optimise the use of natural ventilation, heat, and light, they need to be protected from new development that could overshadow them, obstruct beneficial air flows, or remove valuable shelter. Particular care is required to analyse the shadowing effect of tall buildings, which can influence an open space even when located some distance away. Building cut-off angles can be established and formally adopted as a planning control tool to ensure that new tall buildings are not allowed to overshadow city squares.

When considering a site for a new public space the seasonal movement of the sun needs to be charted across the site, taking account of existing and proposed buildings. A sun path diagram will allow shadow projections to be made for different times of the day and across the seasons, according to the latitude of the site. This analysis will reveal which areas receive direct sunshine at different times, and so help to allocate different uses to their optimum locations.

In most climates, the main open space within the city square should receive direct sunlight during the times of peak use, especially when workers are out to lunch. In temperate climates, far from the equator, it is essential that city squares

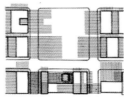

Summer, June 22

Spring, March 21, Autumn, September 23

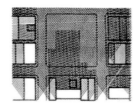

Winter, December 22

Above. A sun path diagram shows how shadows are cast across a site, and where and when direct sunlight will fall. (From Ref. 44, International Thompson Publishing.)

Above. Historic glass canopies in Buxton in the UK provide shelter from the weather and enhance the townscape.

Left. Contemporary canopies in Duke of York Square in London. (Courtesy of Adam Parker Photography.)

receive as much direct sunlight as possible, while shelter from the rain and wind should also be readily available. In hotter and sunnier climates, provision of shade and cool places within the city square will be more important – colonnades are traditionally provided around the edges of squares to meet this need. In the ancient Roman forum in Nîmes in southern France, provision was made for cool promenading areas in semi-submerged vaulted arcades around the edges of the square (which have survived intact today). If colonnades are not a viable option, providing innovative canopy designs around a square – perhaps in canvas or glass – could help to provide a unique identity and provide shelter from the weather.

Studies in Manhattan and Copenhagen revealed that when the temperature is above about 13°C there is a considerable increase in the pleasure derived from walking, standing, or sitting in squares. However, when summer temperatures reach about 24°C some people will find the heat uncomfortable and will seek areas of shelter.[58,59]

Designers also need to be aware of local temperature ranges to ensure that the open space and the buildings around it take account of these variances. The rate of heating and cooling of the surface materials around the city square will be the main factor determining the temperature of the air within the public space. The choice of surface materials within the square and on the buildings around it should therefore be guided by the objective of avoiding extremes of microclimate. Materials need to quickly absorb and store excess heat, and quickly release the heat again when temperatures fall. This will be determined by their physical structure, colour, and surface texture.

Materials such as mirrored glass have a high albedo, i.e. they are highly reflective. They redirect the sun's energy into the microclimate, resulting in temperatures rising quickly within the surrounding area on a warm day, and may also cause dazzling glare. Such a microclimate soon becomes uncomfortable and people will avoid it. To create a pleasant microclimate, reflective materials should therefore be generally avoided, while conductive materials, such as rough stone, are more suitable because they avoid sharp changes in temperature (see *Site Planning*[60] by Lynch and Hack, page 65).

An expanse of paving will significantly increase the reflection of the sun's energy, resulting in higher summer temperatures. The choice of surface stone should therefore be directly influenced by the climatic conditions. Natural vegetation is very effective at reducing this albedo and in balancing the temperature, and therefore soft landscaping, especially trees, should be considered in design proposals for public space to ameliorate the microclimate.

Above. Simple granite paving setts at Covent Garden in London, which last for over 100 years, appear smart, and contribute to a pleasant microclimate.

Wind

Knowing about wind speed is important because it influences temperature and, if too strong, can render a public space unusable. A fairly uniform building height is much less likely to cause adverse wind speeds compared with an irregular one, and high-rise buildings can be particularly problematic. This is because very tall buildings tend to deflect wind downwards, multiplying its force and making conditions at ground level uncomfortable. Estimating the effects of wind on the microclimate within a city square is more difficult and uncertain than for sunshine. If there is a risk of inappropriate wind conditions, a wind tunnel model can be used to experiment with possible solutions.

Above. Wind forces can be deflected by high-rise buildings, with unpleasant effects for the local microclimate.

The effect of wind speed on pedestrians:[3]

WIND SPEED: MPH	PEDESTRIAN DISCOMFORT
> 4	No noticeable effect
4–8	Wind is felt on the face
8–13	Wind disturbs hair and flaps clothing
13–19	Wind raises dust and dry soil and disarranges hair
19–26	The force of the wind is felt on the body
26–34	Umbrellas are used with difficulty, hair is blown straight, and difficulty in walking is experienced

Noise

Perhaps the most intrusive pollutant infringing on the enjoyment of a city square is the noise of motor traffic. Sometimes vehicles cannot be removed and so consideration has to be given to ameliorating the harmful effects of traffic noise. Walls are the most effective sound barriers when they are of solid construction and without any perforation that will let the sound through. However, to be effective they must be sufficiently long and high, and close to the source of the noise or to the people to be protected. Clearly, sound barriers cannot be erected without very careful consideration of their aesthetic effect on a square, and of the effect they will have upon surveillance.

The arrangement of the buildings and landscaping around a square will usually be the most effective and visually appropriate means of controlling sound. Noise can seem louder and more irritating when its source cannot be seen, which means that it may be better to live with the noise than to erect barriers. Alternatively, noise can be softened by the bubbling and gurgling of a water feature. The section on fountains later in this chapter provides more information on water features.

LANDSCAPING

Landscaping has an important role to play in the design of a city square. It can be used to enhance the comfort of users – for example, through the creation of suntraps, areas of shade, wind breaks, and by helping to filter out unwanted noise and unsightly views. It can also be used to stimulate the senses with colour and pleasant scents. Landscaping can also play an important role in emphasising axial sight lines along pedestrian paths within and out of the square. While care is required to ensure that the height and massing of planting does not reduce the legibility of the square, planting can be structured to appear stimulating to people passing through the public space.

The design of landscaped areas needs to ensure that people do not take short cuts through planted areas, or attempt to climb over planters that are inappropriately positioned. A measure of the success of the landscaping scheme will be whether remedial measures have to be taken to protect planting from the square's users at a later date. Close attention to landscaping the subspaces is required to ensure that they stimulate the senses of people who stay in the square for longer periods of time.

When producing a planting programme for a city square, species should ideally be indigenous to the area as these are best adapted to the local climate and can support biodiversity – for example, by attracting insects and birds. Indigenous plant species have the greatest balancing effect on the microclimate and will require the least maintenance. Selecting indigenous species also helps to promote local identity and distinctiveness. When considering which trees to select for different parts of the square, consideration needs to be given to their shapes, rates of growth, potential heights, and pollution resistance.

Special care is required when planting close to building elevations that have been designed for passive solar interaction. Deciduous trees are best located close to these buildings because in the summer, when they are in leaf, they offer welcome shade, and in the winter their bare branches will let the sunlight filter through.

A planting programme that includes fast-growing trees to create an early impact, along with slower growers that will live longer, can help to maintain a population of tall and healthy trees within a square. The trees that grow at the quickest rate will generally be the first to die. Where possible, trees should be surrounded by soft material, such as earth, grass, or mulches, which will enhance their growing environment. If they are surrounded by paving or other hard surfaces, tree pits may be required. The rate of growth and potential height of the tree will be dependent upon the size of these pits. Clearly, trees should not be planted where their roots could damage the foundations of buildings, or where their eventual spread could restrict the light into any principal rooms within buildings facing onto the public space. As a guide, most

Right. Indigenous tree species usually have the greatest balancing effect on the microclimate and require the least maintenance. These trees in Japan add to the local distinctiveness and identity of the area they grow in. (Courtesy of David McDonald.)

forest trees have root systems that are up to 200 per cent larger than the spread of the branches and 90 per cent of the roots will be within the top metre of the soil.[61]

The layering of planting requires careful consideration. For example, dense planting close to the ground can attract litter and vermin, and planting that exceeds a height of 750 mm can provide hiding places for criminal activity. Raised beds or individual planters can be used to effectively display planting at the height of shrubs. Although the plants within planters require greater maintenance, especially when there is either too much or too little rainwater, the planters can be designed to double as seats. These features can be effective in enlivening and softening blank building walls, and can be used to bring colour and pleasant scents to areas where people are sitting.

Planting can be used as a useful behavioural prop – for example, smelling or observing flowers provides something that provides a legitimate reason to be there for people who are simply hanging around in a square for a while. When there are spectacular floral displays to look at, people will congregate around them, and they become a major attraction within public space. Having something to look at, or to physically interact with, appears to be especially important for those who visit a square on their own.

Above. People flocked to see this floral display in Centenary Square in Birmingham – it helped to generate activity within an underused part of the square.

Right. On a hot day in central London, sunbathers occupy almost every square metre of grass in Soho's Golden Square.

Lawn areas are useful when they can be informally used, especially because it is more comfortable to relax on soft grass on sunny days. However, if a square is to retain its urban identity and avoid becoming a park, the lawn areas should not be too expansive. Unless it is a very fine day for sunbathing, people tend to avoid large expanses of grass. The inclusion of grass, trees, and other areas of natural planting, as seen in most of London's residential squares, supports environmental sustainability within the city. Areas of planting produce life-sustaining oxygen from carbon dioxide, provide a natural habitat, and reduce pollution (as the rough surface of leaves hold on to dust particles). Areas of planting allow rainwater to soak into the soil, a process that replenishes the soil water and is essential for life. Hard surface areas usually direct rainwater straight into drains, from where it is taken directly to rivers and eventually the sea.

Urban soils

One of the most serious problems for urban soils is the compaction they suffer from the activities of people, vehicles, and buildings. This compaction reduces the pore space in the soil, which contains the life-giving water and oxygen. Therefore, if buildings have previously occupied a site, the condition of the soil, especially its texture, must be carefully considered and soil tests will be necessary.

The site selected for a new city square will often be a redeveloped 'brownfield' site, and the problem of soil compaction will need to be addressed before any landscaping scheme is considered. One solution is to bring in soil from elsewhere, while another costly option is to inject the existing soil with compressed air. There are a number of other, more sustainable, ways of improving compacted urban soils, although these are likely to take considerable time to work. For example, some plants, such as birch and river alder, have adapted to survive in anaerobic conditions, while other species have strong taproots that create new pore spaces as they penetrate the soil in search of minerals. Mulches and worms can also be applied to urban soils to tackle the compaction and add nutrients. If salt spray has entered the soil from neighbouring roads, this will have to be flushed out – seaweed or gypsum extract can assist with this.

Fountains

The sight and sound of cascading water is a great attraction. The sound of water can be delightful, and helps to drown out undesirable sounds, such as traffic noise. Water creates a special kind of calming ambience, which can bring welcome relief to the stresses of urban life.

Right. A low-pressure jet of water will sparkle in the sunlight and has a pleasant splattering sound that can filter out unwelcome traffic noise, Brindley Place, Birmingham.

When light strikes water at a low angle, it causes light and heat to be directed at waterside objects, which can have significant design implications. For example, glass buildings at the waterside may heat up quickly, resulting in an uncomfortable environment.[48] If there are tall buildings around the square that create strong down winds, a fountain could be impractical due to uncontrollable spray. Before undertaking the detailed design of a fountain, the visual effect and functional qualities that it will offer need to be established. A fine spray has a larger evaporative surface area, which results in a mist and a gentle hum with a pleasant cooling effect. A low-pressure arching jet of water will sparkle in the sunlight and has a pleasant irregular splattering sound.

A fountain combined with sculpture can appear particularly dramatic. A fine example can be seen in William's Square in Las Colinas, Dallas–Fort Worth (Texas), which includes a pool with large bronze wild horses running through it. At the hooves of the horses are fountains, which splash water and emphasise the feeling of movement. The horse is symbolic of the Texas region, and the whole effect of the fountain and sculpture is vigorously dynamic and transforms an otherwise undistinguished square.[44]

Children find water irresistible and safety is therefore an issue, but their joy of interacting with water can be accommodated in a reasonably safe way. High visibility and natural surveillance of water features is essential. Public squares are one of the most secure places for children to safely enjoy water features – if the square is well designed, there will be plenty of people around to offer assistance if any children get into difficulty. One important safety measure is that when the water jets of a fountain are turned off, the water should be clearly visible as being water, and not as a solid surface that can be walked over.

A fountain's main demand on management resources comes from the fact that it has to be turned off and cleaned daily. Special care is required to remove any dangerous articles thrown into the water, especially broken glass.

SEATING PROVISION

William Whyte's study of squares in Manhattan[62] concluded, after three months of extensive research, that there were many factors that had a significant bearing on where people are most likely to sit in a public space – the microclimate and the availability of food, for example. But the most overriding factor was that people are most likely to sit where places have been provided for them to sit!

Many features in a square, such as statues and planters, can be designed for sitting on. If seats are to be well used they need to be orientated for people watching, but there should also be a range of seating provision. For example, seats should be designed to accommodate individuals who want some private space, as well as for groups of people who want to enjoy interacting with each other.

In designing the seating arrangements within a square it is useful to understand people's spatial relationships. Intrusion on an individual's personal space may inhibit their freedom to behave in a relaxed way. The extent of somebody's personal space within a public place is likely to depend on factors such as their personal life experiences, culture, age, gender, and ethnicity, and whether they are alone or are in a group. If they are within a group, their personal space will depend on the total number of people and on how well they know and like each other.[63]

Right. This square in Barcelona shows how seating can be designed to accommodate a variety of users – the space is used by a wide cross section of the community.

In Western culture, personal distance is generally within the range of outstretched arms (approximately 1.2 m), and within this distance, only familiar friends and acquaintances are usually welcomed. Social distance extends from 1.2 to 3.7 m and within this distance nobody usually touches or expects to be touched by another person, and actions are more formal and business-like. Public distance extends beyond 3.7 m, and this is more characteristic of speakers and their audience.[44]

Men have historically dominated public life, and research reveals that men are still likely to dominate certain parts of public space.[64] Both men and women, of all ages, should feel safe and relaxed within a city square, and they should feel that their spatial needs have been accommodated. Research from the USA, including that by Whyte in Manhattan[4] and by Cooper Marcus and Francis in San Francisco,[3] has concluded that men predominate in all kinds of 'up-front' spaces, those that are close to the pedestrian flows, while women prefer more secluded and quieter 'retreat' spaces. Through observing behaviour patterns in the city squares of Birmingham, including Victoria Square, Centenary Square, Chamberlain Square, and Saint Philip's Cathedral Square, it is evident that women are more selective than men about where they will sit. Younger men do sit up-front, as close to the pedestrian flow as possible, and they are also more likely to sit on steps, statue plinths, and almost anything upon which it is possible to sit. They appear to be much more likely to interact physically with artefacts, such as public art, in exposed parts of the square.

Far Left. People like sitting next to pedestrian flows, men seem to predominate in these 'up-front' locations, as shown here in Birmingham's Chamberlain Square.

Left. Young men are most likely to interact physically with artefacts such as public art, as in this example in Victoria Square in Birmingham.

There also appears to be a correlation between the intensity of the pedestrian flow and the distance that people, but especially women, will sit away from it. When the pedestrian flows in a square are low or scattered, few men and very few women will sit there at all, and those that do sit stay close to the pedestrian flow. Conversely, when there are high pedestrian flows, many more people are prepared to sit, and they sit further away from the flow. Sitters attract more sitters, and as such there appears to be a human multiplier effect. Men generally dominate in the up-front locations in Birmingham's squares, and when women sit they are observed to be nearly always within close proximity and within direct sight and sound of the main pedestrian flows.

Within Birmingham's squares, women could only be seen in retreat locations when they were in young mixed couples, and occasional groups of three or more young women (especially teenagers) would sit up to 15 m away from a pedestrian flow. During a hot lunch break, when many sunbathers filled the open lawn areas in Saint Philip's Cathedral Square, individual working women seemed happy to sit further from the pedestrian flow, but they would still remain less than 5 m from another group of sitters, which nearly always included at least one other woman. It is predominantly only older men who appear to sit in 'retreat' locations, more than 15 or 20 m away from the main pedestrian flows.

The different behaviour patterns of men and women and of different age groups within different cultural contexts have implications on the design of seating within public spaces. To encourage social inclusion there should be a variety of seating provision to cater for all legitimate users, whether they visit the square alone or in small groups. It is especially important to include seating next to busy pedestrian flows because the majority of men and women will want to sit there. It is also helpful to provide alternative, improvised seating, especially for younger people. When they climb up to different levels to find a perch they help to create an animated scene.

Steps can be designed to accommodate movement and rest, or both. A steep change of levels in Birmingham's Chamberlain Square has been arranged into a crescent of steps, which resembles an amphitheatre. These steps successfully accommodate both movement and rest and result in an animated scene at different levels. The dimensions of the steps appear to be a critical factor, and in Chamberlain Square the treads measure 380 mm in width and the risers are 145 mm in height. The combination of these measurements means that anyone between five and six feet tall can sit on one step and rest their feet on a lower step, with knees comfortably in front of the body. The steps in Chamberlain Square are particularly effective for accommodating speakers and their audiences, and the crescent layout reinforces this. The performer can use both the base of the square and the steps themselves, while the audience sits on the steps around them.

Above. The steps in Birmingham's Chamberlain Square are well designed for sitting, and meetings are regularly held upon them.

Top Right. The gentler rise of the steps in Victoria Square in Birmingham makes them easier to run up and down, but less effective for sitting.

Bottom Right. Businessmen from the City of London seek quiet 'retreat' space during their lunch breaks.

In Birmingham's redesigned Victoria Square the steps beside the cascading fountain are more clearly designed for movement. The treads of the steps are wider, being between 460 and 560 mm, and are lower, with risers being just 130 mm high. The gentler rise makes the steps easier to run up and down, but the greater width means that if anybody sits on them they have to tuck their knees very close to their body with feet resting on the same step that they are sitting on, or alternatively, legs have to be stretched out in an uncomfortable way to rest feet on the next step down. Because both ways of sitting feel awkward, few people sit on these steps. Instead, people sit on the adjacent wall, which forms part of the fountain's structure. This wall is beside the pedestrian flow and is popular for people watching.

Peaceful retreat space within a square appears to be used much more by men or small mixed groups. Smaller individual pod seats may be more appropriate than benches in such locations. This is because seats located further than 15–20 m from a pedestrian flow are far enough away from passers-by to be used for criminal or antisocial activities. Maintaining visual links with the main pedestrian flows is essential for maintaining a sense of safety.

PUBLIC ART

Public art strategies that are well planned and produced through engaging with local people can reflect the objectives and aspirations of the city and assist with urban regeneration. City squares are ideal places for displaying the kinds of art that reflect the collective identity of the urban area, or the wider region. The herd of wild horses that appears to be charging through the fountain in the middle of the William's Square in Dallas–Fort Worth, Texas, achieves this dramatically.

Public art can be used as a key component in the development of an urban design strategy. For example, art can be used to engage with local people in community participation workshops to encourage them to express how they perceive their area. Arts themes can then be developed to become engines for regeneration.

This has happened in North Shields, a redundant fishing port in the north-east of England, where the Freeform Arts group has engaged with local people through arts workshops, resulting in a new theme for regeneration based on the salmon returning to the river Tyne. This has strengthened the town's ties with the fishing industry in a positive way, and has influenced the creation of new works of art, street furniture, a new arts centre, and a new annual festival – the Fish Quay Pageant.

Initiatives such as this help visitors to structure a mental picture of what the area is about, and what its social characteristics and values are. It shows how public art can be used to reflect regeneration objectives and to present the cultural identity of the area positively.

Some artists produce designs that invite controversy because this provides them with publicity, but public art within a city square needs to reflect public taste. It can be used to promote contact and communication between people. Care is therefore required to ensure that public art speaks to a large percentage of the population. There should at least be public consultation regarding new works of art within the public realm, to provide the art with the stamp of approval from the people that will live with it.

Given that city squares are democratic places that promote social inclusion, public art should not be so formally placed as to suggest that the square was designed purely as a backdrop for it. Autocratic dictators developed such squares around statues of themselves!

Art provides an opportunity to explore history and the deeper concerns that are not generally discussed in rushed urban encounters. It can stir the imagination – perhaps drawing on local legend or myth. The meaning of art for children is worth exploring because if they find it interesting, adults probably will too.

Above. 'The Guardians' of Birmingham's Victoria Square were produced as part of a public art strategy designed to reflect the city's multicultural identity.

Public art needs to be highly visible and is best located near to the areas of high pedestrian flow. When artwork can be seen from streets connecting with a square, it will help to encourage visitors to enter the square to see what is going on.

Public art can play a part in demonstrating that the space within a public square is symbolic and representative of the collective values of an urban society. Even before the existence of a settled urban society, there must have been a human desire for active public space – for a symbolic place to gather, where people could be welcomed on common ground. From early Neolithic times to the present day, pilgrimage to the sacred locations of miracles and symbolic events have been an essential part of life for many communities.

Pilgrimage is still practised in Afghanistan, where the 'ziarat' is a small, often ancient, building that celebrates the holy site at the pilgrim's destination. It is decorated with brilliantly coloured banners to identify the spot for pilgrims within the vast, baked countryside. Today, Afghan settlements are based on the traditional Muslim form, where dwellings face away from the street into private courts and high walls face the street, essentially to protect women from public view. Wherever such a village has grown around an ancient ziarat, there is a marked contrast between the ziarat and the rest of the settlement. It has been said of the ziarat that 'its sociability is a visual gift to the traveller and a public expression of community'.[65]

In Britain the ancient wayside crosses were erected on the sites of early mark stones, which were placed at locations associated with legendary heroes and leaders. Some of these sites assumed importance for pilgrims, became Roman altars, open-air courts, places of worship, or sites for the crowning of Saxon Kings, as demonstrated by the Coronation Stone at Kingston upon Thames.[66]

The Coronation Stone can still be seen at Kingston upon Thames, Edward the Elder was crowned upon it on 8 June in the year 900. The carved stone itself appears to be much older and its symbolic significance to earlier communities

Below. This standing stone in Japan carries inscriptions and poems to guide people travelling along an ancient route. (Courtesy of David McDonald.)

Left. Public art can be transformed into local theatre when children can climb over it, as with the lions in Trafalgar Square in London.

can only be guessed at. A solid object such as a stone, which marks space and represents a symbolic function, is a powerful design element, and this remains relevant for public space and art today.

As with the ancient ziarat, public art can be a bright and lively attraction, and as with early mark stones, it can have symbolic connections. The areas around public art need to accommodate people, with plenty of spaces for sitting and looking. The senses should be stimulated. People, and especially children, should be encouraged to be actors in the scene, interacting with public art rather than leaving it as an inanimate object.

Camillo Sitte stated over a hundred years ago that there no longer appears to be an interest in adorning public space. On the proper siting of works of art, he reminds us that Michelangelo's David originally stood exactly where the artist had planned. This was close to the walls of the Palazzo Vecchio in Florence, to the left of the principal entrance. The siting was apparently so ordinary as to appear absurd to Sitte's contemporaries. However, on this site the masterpiece of David appeared to be brooding and 'The enormous statue seems to swell even beyond its actual dimensions'.[46] The statue did not need a central position and did not need to look as if the square had been designed around it.

A common mistake with the siting of public art in squares is that the largest possible space is sought for the smallest of works, this diminishes the effect that the art work could have. A neutral background, such as a simple building, will often be the best setting for public art. Some form of background and context for art works is important, but excessively rich and ornate backgrounds need to be avoided because they compete for the viewers' attention. In the ancient agora and forum, statues were grouped together, and Camillo Site commented that 'This rage for isolating everything is truly a modern sickness'.[46]

Positioning public art is an art in itself. If a piece of work is moved from the position selected for it by the artist, harm is done to both the artwork and its creator. When a new bronze cast was taken from the statue of David it was placed in the mathematical centre of a square off the Via dei Colli. From this new setting the statue produced no effect at all, and Sitte claimed that he heard observers saying its dimensions did not exceed the human stature at all. Camillo Sitte claimed that:[46]

> The location of monuments on the axes of monumental buildings or richly adorned portals should be avoided for it conceals worthwhile architecture from the eyes, and reciprocally, an excessively rich and ornate background is not appropriate for a monument. The ancient Egyptians understood this principle ... for the obelisks and the statues of the pharaohs are aligned beside the temple doors.

Right. The 'Iron Man' in Victoria Square in Birmingham marks space beside a pedestrian flow, but the centrally positioned statue of Queen Victoria merges into the classical detailing of the building behind it.

Far Right. Statues in the far distance draw the eye into the Piazza Della Signoria in Florence, but they do not obstruct pedestrian flows nor compete with the fine architectural detailing.

The ancient Greeks and Romans erected their works of art to the sides of city squares, where the number of statues could increase without obstructing the circulation of traffic, and each statue would have a building to provide an appropriate background. The Roman architect Vitruvius stated that the centre of a public place is destined not for statues, but for gladiators!

Camillo Sitte identified an effective and simple method for siting public art based, surprisingly, on the location of snowmen. To begin with, imagine a city square in winter, covered in snow. Pathways will have been beaten across the square in line with established pedestrian flows. Between these pathways remain large blocks of undisturbed snow. Here, the snowmen are built, 'for that is where the substance of which they are made is found'.[46] This methodology helps to explain why statues are traditionally arranged differently in different squares. The arrangement and siting of statues should reflect the patterns of movement that occur through the space.

To summarise, the edges of public squares are often the most appropriate places for art works because the works will have suitable backgrounds, be out of the paths of traffic, leave robust spaces in the middle of the square for other activities and events, and, by being close to pedestrian flows and building entrances, be guaranteed an audience. Caution is required if a symmetrical or geometric positioning of public art is being considered as the art work can become an obstacle, and the formal layout is often only appreciated from a single raised viewpoint.

The importance of behaviour props has already been mentioned, and public art should be something for people to attach themselves to – to sit on or lean against. Public art contributes to activity within the square when it provides people with a legitimate reason to be there and to linger for a while. A time-lapse study of 6,000 users in ten Vancouver squares found that less than one per cent of people carried out any activities in the open, away from any physical artefacts or props (such as public art).[67]

Below. People like to place themselves near something – be it a bench, pillar, or sculpture – as shown here at Brindley Place in Birmingham.

LIGHTING

Artificial lighting of the city square during the hours of darkness is clearly essential for security and for facilitating the night-time economy, but lighting can also be used to artistic effect – to provide the square with a special night-time character.

Lighting within modern cities has become preoccupied with accommodating the requirements of motorised transport, but this kind of lighting is the antithesis of that which creates a pleasant place for people. Most standard lighting columns are of an intimidating scale, being between 8 and 12 m in height, to provide for maximum horizontal illumination across a road surface. It is due to a combination of these regularly positioned columns and to poorly designed sodium fixtures that our cities are consumed by a monotonous orange glow at night-time. Pedestrian-friendly lighting columns are no more than 5 m in height – beneath this height they appear to be of a reasonable human scale. The standard height for highway lighting columns creates a 'Colditz effect' in public spaces.

Although blanket sodium lighting was developed for highway illumination, it is also commonly used to illuminate pedestrian streets and squares. This kind of lighting appears alien in the pedestrian environment, and it drains images of their natural colour and detail. Sodium lighting is best avoided within a city square and in any pedestrian streets that connect with it (in fact, it is best avoided everywhere). White light provided by metal halide or modern fluorescents is superior and provides good colour rendering, which enables people to see true colours at night-time.

Consultant lighting designers are increasingly available to join multidisciplinary teams and produce lighting strategies that can improve the image of the city after dark. These lighting strategies can ensure that a city's unique spaces and buildings are illuminated to great effect, adding to local character and distinctiveness. Lighting is especially important at visual gateways into the city, into its various quarters, along strategic routes, and within its city squares.

The image of city squares at night can be dramatically improved through the illumination of vertical rather than horizontal surfaces. This involves directing light at objects within a pedestrian's field of vision, such as buildings, landscaping, or public art, and being less preoccupied with illuminating the ground surface. A pleasant ambience can be created with indirect lighting, including the underlighting of soft landscaping, fountains, and architectural features. Lighting can also be used to enhance the texture of the materials within a square – for example, lighting at an angle will emphasise the roughness of a surface that, if lit square on, would appear smooth.

Above. Skilled lighting engineers were key members of the project management team that delivered improvements to Kensington High Street in London. (Courtesy of Royal Borough of Kensington and Chelsea/Project Centre Ltd/Woodhouse.)

While lighting equipment needs to be designed and positioned to resist vandalism, theft, and corrosion, it is an integral part of the street furniture within the city square and therefore needs to be of a high-quality design. Discrete spot lighting fixtures attached directly onto buildings can help to reduce clutter and leave robust space within the square.

'Sky glow' is a visually intrusive form of light pollution, which wastes electricity, money, and the earth's finite energy resources. Whole generations have grown up in cities without ever seeing the vivid splendour of bright stars against a dark night sky, and yet this could be easily remedied by a more-considered approach to lighting design. Sky glow can be easily avoided by directing light downwards wherever possible, to illuminate its target rather than the night sky, or by ensuring that light fittings are shielded to prevent light spilling above the horizontal, and ideally within 70 degrees from the vertical.[68]

Through creating a contrast in the intensity of light, and by illuminating special features within the city, different areas become visually distinct. This can assist way-finding and orientation at night-time. To create a stimulating night-time image within the city square, uniformity of illumination should be avoided.

Given the significance of night-time illumination, a lighting strategy should form an integral part of an urban design strategy, and this should be produced by qualified lighting designers in liaison with urban designers. A lighting plan has been produced and implemented in Trafalgar Square, where the night-time character has been transformed and important buildings are shown to best effect. Light glare has been reduced and the night sky over the square remains relatively dark. Light strategies have been produced for whole cities, perhaps with greatest success in Lyon in France, where at night the city sparkles like a jewel enveloped in darkness.

CASE STUDY

THE PLACA REIAL IN BARCELONA: A CASE STUDY

The Placa Reial in Barcelona, Spain, was built in the 1840s and demonstrates an almost complete sense of enclosure, with six of its seven entry points being located behind colonnades. The colonnades minimise the breakage in the building line around the square and reinforce a strong architectural composition.

The principal access point into the Placa Reial represents the only break in the built frontage around the square. This opening is provided with architectural emphasis to reinforce the sense of a visual gateway onto the processional route of La Rambla.

Apart from the break caused by this visual gateway, the colonnades run continuously around the square. The space under the colonnades measures approximately 5 m in width and 8 m in height. This semi-enclosed area provides a sheltered and lofty subspace in between the enclosed shops and the open square. The space fills with cafe tables and is an ideal place for people watching. Curtains are pulled down between the columns when it is too hot or raining.

Right. Providing access points into the Placa Reial from underneath buildings and from behind colonnades helps to create a uniform sense of enclosure within the square.

Far Right. Inviting shopfronts and cafes around the Placa Reial provide a sense of surveillance underneath the colonnades, but antisocial behaviour occurs when security roller shutters result in blind walls.

In order to retain a sense of surveillance under the colonnades when the cafes are closed, it is vital that the shopfronts are designed as windows onto the public realm. In parts of the Placa Reial, security roller shutters are pulled down over shop windows when the cafes shut, and in these areas the colonnades soon attract antisocial activity. It would be better if internal shutters were used, especially if they were perforated to remain visually transparent – to at least provide a perception of surveillance from within.

Above the colonnades are regularly spaced balconies at first- and second-floor levels. These balconies establish horizontal rhythms around the square and provide a sense of activity and surveillance. The first-floor level is provided with architectural emphasis and serves as the *piano nobile*, with a diminishing scale in the stories above. The top of the building is finished with a strong dentilled cornice and stone balustrading that greets the sky (except where a few unfortunate roof extensions meet the sky in a clumsy and irregular way).

The Placa Reial is a large square, measuring approximately 100 m by 70 m, and the sense of enclosure created through the uniformity of its five-storey buildings is satisfying. The ground-floor colonnades serve as an architectural plinth or base for these buildings. Above the colonnades, the double height Corinthian pilasters define the main body of the buildings.

Left. The coherent architectural composition and appropriate sense of enclosure around the Placa Reial.

The ground surface within the Placa Reial is finished with a simple stone paving, and most of the lighting is fixed to the surrounding buildings to leave a robust open space. There are several decorative lamp standards, which were specially designed by Antoni Gaudi and are features in their own right. There are also several palm trees within the square, which pleasantly contrast with the formal lines of the architecture, and a centrally positioned fountain serves as a focal point and a natural meeting place. The open space within the square accommodates a range of uses, including a market, and the occasional unofficial football match, which many local people are often keen to participate in. The square serves as a gathering place and focal point for the local community, much like a village green.

The Placa Reial benefits from the fact that most of its connecting streets run straight and narrow, with tall buildings on either side. This provides a spatial contrast and makes the open space of the square appear all the more dramatic. This effect is exploited through providing architectural emphasis in the design of corner buildings, especially to reinforce the sense of a visual gateway into the square from the connecting processional route of La Rambla.

The design and uses of the buildings around the square play a crucial role in creating activity. Building density is relatively high and accommodates large numbers of people, who assist in generating activity and surveillance. The upper floors of the buildings around the Placa Reial are in residential use – the apartments are accessed from communal stairwells that include well-designed ground-floor entrances that open directly onto the square.

Building density has to be balanced with creating an appropriate sense of enclosure and preventing overdevelopment. When buildings are below six storeys in height, as in the Placa Reial, they are of a particularly robust form because they can often operate without elevators, which is one measure towards creating an environmentally sustainable building form.

PERFORMANCE CHECKS: PHYSICAL FORM AND ROBUSTNESS

- Has consideration been given to connecting main squares with processional routes?
- Have landmarks or other design features been included to show how different squares fit into the local hierarchy of public spaces?
- Has consideration been given to providing a range of different squares with various sizes to accommodate different functions and uses?
- Have the buildings, landscaping, subspaces, and other design components in each square combined to form a visually stimulating composition that is greater than the sum of its parts?
- Have public buildings and art been properly integrated into design proposals for public space?
- Has sufficient space been provided for events, movement, and rest, and have the needs of different kinds of people in public space been addressed?
- Have residential units been included around squares above ground level to provide a sense of surveillance, activity, and community upkeep. Do the residential units have well-designed entry points onto public space?
- Have key entry points into squares, from adjoining streets, been given visual emphasis, for example through the design of distinctive corner buildings and careful location of attractions?
- Have engineers and designers collaborated to ensure public space is uncluttered and that lighting is considered as an art form?

CHAPTER FOUR>

CHAPTER FOUR
RENAISSANCE IN BIRMINGHAM

BIRMINGHAM

The city of Birmingham is centrally located at the heart of England, where it serves as the regional capital for the West Midlands. It is the second largest city in the UK, with a population of over one million within its administrative boundary, and it sits within an urban conurbation of over five million people. Birmingham provides an example of how effective leadership and a successful urban design strategy can focus investment to create new and improved city squares and interconnected streets that can transform a city and its region.

In the 19th century, Birmingham had benefited from a visionary mayor, Joseph Chamberlain, who was elected to the Council in 1869 and went on to implement municipal improvements on a grand scale. Much of the city had been in a squalid condition prior to his administration. Chamberlain himself said that before his time Birmingham was '... badly lighted, imperfectly guarded, and only partially drained; there were few public buildings and few important streets ... But now great public edifices not unworthy of the importance of a Midland metropolis have risen on every side. Rookeries and squalid courts have given way to fine streets and open places. The roads are well paved, well kept, well lighted, and well cleansed ... Free libraries and museums of art are open to all the inhabitants'. Chamberlain also said 'I have an abiding faith in municipal institutions ... an abiding sense of the value and importance of local self-government, and I desire therefore to surround them by everything which can mark their importance'.[69]

Chamberlain's legacy has survived to an extent, but Birmingham suffered greatly through war damage, post-war redevelopment, and highway engineering that had little regard to wider environmental or social issues. The city had developed as a significant industrial town in the 18th century, growing rapidly, with a traditional pattern of streets and squares arranged in an irregular grid pattern. It became known around the world as the city of a thousand trades. The city later suffered from the collapse of its manufacturing industry in the 1970s. Employment in the city fell by 29 per cent between 1971 and 1983 (Birmingham City Council figures).

Much of the post-war redevelopment of the city contrasted with the earlier irregular grid pattern, and was primarily designed in the 1960s for motor vehicle accessibility. This resulted in the construction of a number of ring roads, including the inner ring road, now recognised as being a 'concrete collar' around the city centre. The ring roads sliced through the traditional urban blocks, leaving a fragmented urban structure and a confused public realm. The backs of buildings and car parks often faced public spaces and streets, resulting in dead frontages and a lack of natural surveillance.

At the end of the 1980s the sparks of municipal leadership began to ignite again, and slowly but surely much of the neglect in the city centre has been turned around. Through implementing an urban design strategy, Birmingham is now well embarked upon an urban renaissance of a scale unknown since the time of Chamberlain. The strategy has transformed a car-dominated city centre, which

Right. Plan of Birmingham's traditional deformed grid pattern in 1861. (Courtesy of Birmingham City Council)

Far Right. Plan of Birmingham in 1990. Post-war planning to accommodate car use had resulted in a broken and fragmented layout. (Courtesy of Birmingham City Council)

was blighted by high unemployment, into an attractive place where tourism, education, international conferences, the arts, and high-technology industries are thriving alongside state-of-the-art shopping and city centre housing. The change in the city's fortunes indicates the importance of urban design for regeneration. The strategy has also shown how urban squares can be used to market a city, and to increase its standing within the international marketplace.

While accommodating the motor car had been the principal goal of city planning in Birmingham in the 1960s, thirty years later it was realised that while roads were necessary, they must not become barriers to pedestrian movement nor barriers to important views. Through sacrificing pedestrian permeability and the legibility of the built environment to the car, Birmingham could not fully realise its potential as the second city of the UK, or as a major European destination for shopping, business, tourism, and the arts. It became clear to the city council that the physical structure of the city centre would have to be improved if Birmingham were to be successful in changing its image.

CITY CENTRE DESIGN STRATEGY

In 1988, Birmingham City Council and its consultants organised an international design symposium, the 'Highbury Initiative', to address the city's problems. This brought together local interests and international expertise, and it was agreed that the city should define a new role for itself as an international city. Flagship projects for accommodating major events were proposed, including the International Convention Centre and the National Indoor Arena, and there were plans for major new and improved city squares, including Victoria Square, Centenary Square, and Brindley Place, all of which provide a sequential urban design experience. These proposals formed part of a single vision, contained within a comprehensive strategy called the 'City Centre Design Strategy'. The strategy document was produced for the city by consultants Tibbalds, Colbourne, Karski, Williams and was published in 1990.[70]

The strategy developed the idea that the central part of the city contains distinct 'quarters', which are of a homogenous or potentially homogenous character. The strategy states that this character derives from 'the uses, height, scale and bulk of buildings; colour; materials and textures; topography; edges; roof profiles; landscape; landmarks; and so on'. An important section of the strategy identifies the salient characteristics of these areas so their uniqueness can be enhanced in new development proposals. This section of the strategy has helped to focus development control powers properly.

The City Centre Design Strategy was adopted as official supplementary planning guidance and was incorporated into Birmingham's Unitary Development Plan 1993, which provided a statutory basis for planning control in the city.

The design strategy sought to improve the accessibility of the various quarters, which had been cut off from the city centre by the inner ring road (the concrete collar). As several sections of the ring road had been built considerably above ground level it often restricted pedestrian access and views between the different quarters. In comparison with the central area, the quarters were inactive and poorly maintained due to their inadequate pedestrian access and legibility.

To improve pedestrian access and the legibility of the various quarters, it was proposed that the inner ring road be partly re-graded as a ground-level boulevard with ground-level pedestrian crossing points. This would help to spread the city-centre activity into the quarters, and the quarters would accommodate new international facilities, including major retail developments.

It was recognised that if the quarters were to be lively and successful, they must have direct and pleasant pedestrian links with the surrounding urban structure. Links with the core area would be especially important, but there should also be links between neighbouring quarters.

The strategy focused on the delivery of new and improved city squares, and international venues for major events, to the western side of the city centre. These squares have enhanced the identity and distinctiveness of the quarters they are located in, and they have provided new pedestrian links between the quarters. Successful development of the west side of the city centre provided the confidence to tackle the east side of the city, towards Digbeth. This area had become run down and seedy and was becoming increasingly characterised by criminal activity.

WEST-SIDE STORY

The first strategic pedestrian link to be created was from the main railway station at New Street to Brindley Place. This link now serves as an important pedestrian route. Brindley Place is a new square at the heart of a redeveloped quarter, the Broad Street Redevelopment Area, which is located beyond the inner ring road to the west of the city centre.

The Highbury Initiative and subsequent City Centre Design Strategy had proposed that the Broad Street Redevelopment Area be developed as a premier location for conferences, tourism, and leisure in the city. These were identified as growth industries, which could create jobs and wealth to replace the city's lost manufacturing base. This quarter has now been successfully developed, with new city squares, and pedestrian links that connect with the high pedestrian flows of the city centre.

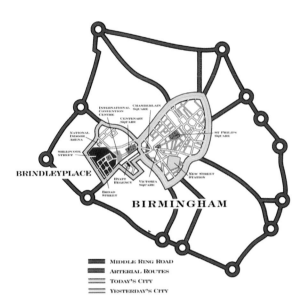

Left. The strategic link between Birmingham's New Street railway station and Brindley Place, in the redeveloped Broad Street Quarter. (Brindleyplace plc.)

Above. The sense of arrival at Victoria Square. (Courtesy of The Salmon Picture Library.)

Five public squares have been created or improved along the new strategic link between the New Street railway station and Brindley Place and the interconnecting streets have been pedestrianised. These improvements provide pedestrians with a sequential experience of interconnected public spaces. The carefully considered landscaping and public art within the squares help to populate the scene with large numbers of people at different levels, and the viewer is continually led onwards to new delights.

After leaving New Street railway station and turning west, New Street provides a direct axial route to the first square in the sequence, Victoria Square. There is a dramatic sense of arrival when the pedestrian leaves New Street and arrives in this irregularly shaped public space. Prior to the improvement works, Victoria Square was little more than a traffic island, with traffic congestion on three sides. This was considered inappropriate for a civic space defined by splendid Victorian buildings, including the grade I listed Council House (in the style of a Venetian palace), a town hall that rises like the ancient Greek Parthenon, and a former post office in the style of a French chateau.

Victoria Square demonstrates how local authorities can design and develop squares when there is clear leadership, vision, and cross-departmental working practices. Inspired by the principles in the City Centre Design Strategy, the transformation of Victoria Square began with a brief produced by the council's City

Centre Planning Team. This provided a vision for a prestigious, pedestrianised civic square. The works were completed in 1993, when the square became a flagship for the city's urban design strategy.

The brief required that public art be an integral part of the redesign for Victoria Square, and that a water feature be included to dramatically exploit the gradient difference within the site. Space was to be provided for rest, and for movement diagonally across the square that follows the pedestrian desire line – on the route from the station to the new quarter off Broad Street. The brief also required that the square be designed to include a robust space for civic events and for informal street entertainment, and that the image of the square reflect the civic importance of the enclosing buildings.

The requirements of the brief have been implemented through cooperation between various teams within the city council. The council's Landscape Practice Group managed the detailed design, while the City Engineer's department undertook contracting and site management. A public art adviser was appointed to produce a coordinating strategy for new commissions, and a lead artist was appointed to develop a unifying artistic concept, which was to become the 'river' group. The public art has been designed and positioned to support human interaction, and people can often be seen climbing, sitting, or propping themselves up on it.

The brief was implemented through a design that included two massive flights of steps with a cascading fountain in between. The fountain is centred on the axis of the facade of the square's principal building, the Council House. It effectively exploits the south–north gradient rise across the site, which is approximately 5 m in height. The steps are finished in high-quality stone paving. They are designed to accommodate fast-moving pedestrian flows by being wide and with low risers. Seating is provided beside the steps, along the retaining walls of the fountain, providing an ideal perch for people watching.

The vertical combination of movement and rest, both of people and water, appears dramatic and appealing when entering the square from New Street. The redesigned square also provides an impressive setting for the council's municipal buildings. The new steps and fountain have facilitated the creation of two level subspaces or terraces out of the sloping site, each measuring approximately 50 m by 30 m. These are robust spaces, the upper level is often used for civic events, while the lower space merges into New Street and is used for more informal entertainment. As a practical alternative to climbing the steps across the square, the ground is shaped along the western corner of the square in a way that facilitates even faster moving pedestrian flows – this route is favoured by commuters in the rush hour.

Clay paviours are laid across the subspaces in a herringbone pattern, which is strong enough to take the heavy vehicle loading necessary to accommodate major events. Street furniture, including lighting, seating, bins, etc., has been specially designed for the square and is carefully positioned for maximum usage without infringing upon robust open space.

The second public space in the sequence is the steeply sloping Chamberlain Square, which connects with the north-western corner of Victoria Square. Although this square has not received anything like the improvements to Victoria Square, it nonetheless provides an important and unusual link.

Chamberlain Square is another irregularly shaped public space, and it measures approximately 75 m by 75 m, with four streets connecting to it. The square is defined by the classical town hall, the side of the Council House, and the city museum and art gallery; as well as by a modernist city library and the Paradise Forum retail mall. The gradient rise from the south to the north is about 6 m, and this has been designed to include both steps and a shaped slope. Similar to Victoria Square, the shaped slope provides a fast moving pedestrian channel that continues the route from the railway station to Brindley Place.

Left. Birmingham's central library and art gallery are major public buildings located on Chamberlain Square – they help to fill the square with people.

The steps are steep and have a sunny aspect facing south. They are arranged around a circular terrace to form a kind of amphitheatre. Many people sit on these steps, especially because the public library and art gallery attract so many young people. The steps are close enough to the pedestrian flow to enjoy people watching without getting in the way.

While the flat terrace area at the base of the steps forms a natural stage, it has poor loadbearing strength due to an underground car park and so major events are restricted. Informal public speaking and entertainers have traditionally occupied the stage area, but recently a large television screen has been erected within it, and its broadcasts appear to have diminished the social interactions. A fountain still stands in the circular terrace at the bottom of the steps and serves as a visual focal point. The fountain is a monument to Joseph Chamberlain, who did so much to strengthen the civic identity of the city. The fountain generates activity, especially by children, who are usually either perched around it or, on hot summer days, playing in it.

The pedestrian route to Brindley Place continues through the rather shabby

Below. A model of the scheme planned in the 1930s for the site of Centenary Square – the unified frontage could have created a better sense of enclosure.

Below Right. The new pedestrian bridge that carries people over the lowered inner ring road and provides access to the new Centenary Square.

Bottom Right. The central position of the sculpture in Centenary Square meant that it was effectively 'lost' in the space. Local people burned it down, and the plinth now serves as a skateboard park. An almost identical sculpture is better located beside a pedestrian flow in Montreal, as shown on page 139.

Paradise Forum mall, which connects with the north-western corner of Chamberlain Square, and out over a new, wide, pedestrian bridge, into the third major public space in the sequence – Centenary Square.

This part of the route was previously bisected by the concrete collar of the inner ring road. Through implementing the urban design strategy, the inner ring road was lowered beneath the new pedestrian bridge so that motor vehicles, rather than people, are forced to change levels. Without these improvement works, the new squares and the Broad Street Quarter would have remained isolated – severed from the central area by traffic.

Pushing vehicles, rather than people, underground has also reduced the harmful effects of pollution and noise, and has facilitated removal of a foreboding system of pedestrian subways. At ground level these improvements have resulted in a new, pleasant pedestrian environment, with direct pedestrian links and a visually stimulating interconnected sequence of public squares. Centenary Square, the third major public space in the sequence, was developed in 1991, soon after the Highbury Initiative. It is a large open space that serves the distinct purpose of being the city's main events space. Although the square is broken up into four manageable subspaces, its total dimensions are approximately 200m by 45m – it can therefore accommodate very large events.

Activity is generated in Centenary Square by pedestrians, who use it as the main route between the city centre and Brindley Place. Activity is also generated by the surrounding buildings, which include Birmingham's Repertory Theatre, the International Convention Centre, Symphony Hall, offices, a Hyatt hotel, and a wedding registry office.

However, the activity is insufficient to cover such a vast square and the broken, poorly defined building frontage adds to the lack of an appropriate sense of enclosure. Broad Street also bisects the square along its length, and the heavy traffic adds to a sense of severance. A controversial sculpture was poorly located in the middle of the square – until local people burned it down. The plinth for the sculpture remains and serves as a skateboard park, which generates a dynamic sense of activity and keeps young people within a safe distance of pedestrian flows.

Below. This sculpture, in Montreal, is almost the same as the one that was sited in Centenary Square. The Montreal one works better because it is located beside a pedestrian flow, rather than in the middle of a square.

Above. The site of the Broad Street Quarter prior to redevelopment. (Brindleyplace plc.)

Right. Brindley Place now forms the focal point of Birmingham's new Broad Street Quarter.

In the 1930s, an interesting urban design scheme was proposed for the area now occupied by Centenary Square, with classically inspired Portland stone buildings of a uniform scale that better related to a civic square. Although a few of the buildings proposed in the scheme were built, a lack of organisation and funds, and the impact of the Second World War, appear to have ruined the vision for the project.

From Centenary Square, the pedestrian route continues through another semi-public mall, the International Convention Centre – which internalises activity in an unfortunate way – and then it continues out across a canal to the new Broad Street Quarter, which contains Brindley Place. While the City Centre Design

Strategy provided the vision and set the principles for the new Broad Street Quarter, Terry Farrell and Co. Architects produced a detailed master plan for the area, including the focal point of Brindley Place. Once the city council had assembled and packaged the redundant industrial sites within the quarter, a private company, Brindleyplace plc, was established to develop the sites on a commercial basis. A dynamic new quarter has now been developed within the Broad Street Redevelopment Area. Although this area has taken about ten years to build, the City Centre Design Strategy managed to help boost confidence in this part of Birmingham soon after its publication in 1990.

There are two new public squares within the Broad Street Quarter, with cafes, offices, and leisure facilities around them. There is also a new housing development nearby. The mile-long stretch of canal side that runs through the quarter has also been exploited and enhanced. The new squares form an important part of the character of the quarter and have enhanced both its legibility and local identity.

There are some recurring problems within Birmingham's new squares, especially in the Broad Street Quarter. For example, although there is a new strategic pedestrian link from the city centre, the squares still rely on being destination points in their own rights, rather than being well integrated within surrounding pedestrian movement patterns. This is partly due to the severance caused by past transport planning mistakes. (Feasibility studies are now being prepared to see if a new underground train network, with stations at key public spaces, should be provided to address this issue.) To a certain extent, squares such as Brindley Place succeed in creating the feel of lively people-places for a large part of the day – this is because of the major visitor attractions and employment uses located around them.

Brindley Place was developed with an objective of providing over one million square feet of office space for corporate headquarters, and so, as a result of this, office space dominates the square. When these offices are closed, the square is conspicuously quiet and requires surveillance by security guards and video cameras. Although new squares such as Brindley Place were advertised as being mixed-use developments, the 140 residential units that form part of the project are located in a separate gated development, off the square and on the other side of a canal. The absence of a residential community within the buildings around the square itself results in a lack of natural surveillance and self-policing of the public realm. It also results in an absence of the natural vitality and sense of community ownership associated with traditional European squares, where buildings accommodate both employment and residential uses and are thereby occupied day and night.

The segregation of uses as seen at Brindley Place is often a requirement of the financial investment companies that usually buy the buildings produced in major development projects. It is based on a belief that segregation of uses makes for effective management. This appears to be a misconception that results in buildings being empty for more hours than they are occupied – and also results in greatly increased security costs. While residential uses have been included above commercial uses in some new squares in the UK, including Gloucester Green in Oxford and Tower Bridge Plaza in London, creating real mixed use remains difficult, and commercial investors still need to be convinced of the merits of mixed-use buildings.

Another problem with the Broad Street Quarter has been the large number of bars that were approved in a relatively concentrated area, especially along Broad Street and fronting the canal side beside Brindley Place. These bars were encouraged to complement the international tourist and business facilities in the quarter, but are in fact mainly used by young people from across the region. Visitors to Birmingham's hotels located off Brindley Place arrive on a Friday or Saturday evening and find they will have to negotiate their way through hoards of revellers, which has resulted in an image problem. It is the concentration of zones of single uses, be it bars or offices, in one area that appears to exacerbate problems that would normally be more diluted within traditional mixed-use urban areas.

Notwithstanding these problems, the housing scheme off Brindley Place provided the first opportunity for relatively wealthy urban pioneers to live within Birmingham's city centre. Prior to the publication of the City Centre Design Strategy there had been no post-war private housing development within Birmingham's city centre. The Brindley Place housing proved that there was a demand for a range of housing types within the city centre, and many new residential schemes are now being developed over commercial premises elsewhere in the city centre. These developments are helping to create a livelier, safer, and more sustainable, urban environment.

Many car-dominated cities in Europe and North America find themselves in a similar position to Birmingham's prior to publication of its City Centre Design Strategy. However, once they begin to invest in new people-friendly public spaces, they also find buoyant markets for homes in their city centres. A central address located by a fashionable square is increasingly popular, both for business and living space. This is the case in old cities such as Copenhagen in Denmark, but also in modern cities such as Toronto in Canada.

Implementing Birmingham's urban design strategy to the west of the city centre has helped to focus investment into creating new public spaces, which have helped Birmingham to win contracts to hold major world events. In 1998, the

Left. The urban design framework produced for Birmingham's Eastside. (Courtesy of Birmingham City Council.)

Above. Birmingham's Eastside prior to redevelopment – dominated by flyovers and car parks. (Courtesy of Birmingham City Council.)

Above Right. Birmingham's Eastside area after removal of the flyovers. New ground-level boulevards are being created.

quarter around Brindley Place hosted the G8 summit of the world's wealthiest industrialised nations. World leaders, including the President of the USA, made use of the restaurants, bars, and leisure facilities, around Birmingham's new squares – as well as the new conference halls. The reward for successfully managing this event was a world marketing opportunity, which the city council embraced to the full. In the year after this event, Birmingham attracted 42 per cent of the entire UK conference market business.[21] To attract major international events, it has been essential for Birmingham to provide appropriate facilities within a well-designed physical environment – a factor of increasing importance as cities bid against each other to hold prestigious international events.

Producing an urban design strategy that includes the vision for city squares and interconnected streets has helped to put Birmingham firmly on the world map.

THE EASTSIDE

Following the successful development of Birmingham's new quarters in the west side of the city centre, the city council produced a new urban design framework to develop the 'Eastside' in a way that builds on the City Centre Design Strategy. This required another break in the raised inner ring road, which has now been transformed into a ground-level boulevard that provides pedestrian access to the new quarters in the east. The new eastern quarters are focused on an area

Right. The viewing terrace at the new Selfridges store.

occupied by the University of Aston, the historic but neglected Digbeth area, and large expanses of surface car parks, cement works, and waste-transfer stations.

The regeneration themes for the new quarters in Eastside are based upon learning, cultural heritage, technology, and state-of-the-art retailing. Birmingham City Council has again worked in partnership with the private sector to develop these areas. The council is one of the main landowners in the area, but it has also used its compulsory purchase powers to create development sites. Various consortia of private investors and developers formed to develop these packaged sites. The city council is now striving to make Eastside an example of how to create an urban renaissance in a way that reflects current urban design thinking (as discussed in the report of the Urban Task Force, chaired by Lord Rogers).[72]

The urban design framework is proposed to unfold with new quarters that contain developments around new public squares, interconnected streets, and a major new city park. Existing traffic nodes, which stand close to the boundary of the city's core area and Eastside, have been transformed into new city squares at ground level to create impressive pedestrian gateways into Eastside.

New interconnected squares, public spaces, vistas, and malls have been created in the flagship Bullring redevelopment. This has replaced a 1960s shopping centre to the east of the city centre that stood upon an island site, surrounded by several lanes of traffic. Pedestrians could only reach the old Bullring centre through a maze of forbidding subways. Shopping streets within the city centre, which provide access to the Bullring area, were pedestrianised in earlier enhancement schemes, and more recently the road junctions approaching the Bullring were transformed by removal of subways, widening of pavements, and provision of ground-level pedestrian crossings. The key difference between the old 1960s Bullring shopping centre and the site as redeveloped is that it now includes public spaces that are interconnected with the pre-existing pedestrian routes, and views of existing and new landmarks have been opened up – the Bullring has been made a legible part of the city centre.

The new department store by architects Future Systems, which is covered in 15,000 spun-aluminium discs, is a brash and dramatic new landmark within the Bullring redevelopment. The new landmark building is no bigger in scale than other new buildings in the redevelopment, but a jelly-mould shape and startling materials make it very distinctive. The building has served as a positive marketing tool for the city, but has resulted in some problems at street level, especially where it presents blind walls to the pavement.

Below. Saint Martin's church in the foreground and the new Selfridges department store by architects Future Systems in the background. (Courtesy of Jonathan Berg/bplphoto.co.uk.)

The city council provided the vision for the new Bullring to fully exploit the potential of existing landmarks – these being the modern icon building of the Rotunda and the parish church of Saint Martin's. The visual impact of these buildings has been maximised by creating a new square around Saint Martin's church and by providing a new wide street that connects from this square to the Rotunda. The Rotunda stands upon the main shopping area of New Street, and a new public space has been created at its base. A new bronze sculpture of a bull, symbolising the cattle market that gave the area its name, has been included in this space.

The Rotunda stands on ground that is significantly higher than the ground level around Saint Martin's church. As such, if you stand on the new public space at the base of the Rotunda and look down the new axial route to Saint Martin's church, the view of the church and the city beyond is dramatic. This view existed in the historic street layout that was destroyed in the 1960s to make way for the modernist Bullring. Today, in the new development, the open view between the spire of Saint Martin's church and the Rotunda is all the more powerful as the two landmarks appear to be in conversation with each other (which is reminiscent of the way that Nelson's Column in London's Trafalgar Square is visually aligned with the route of Whitehall to connect with Big Ben at the Palace of Westminster).

Along the axial line that connects the landmarks of Saint Martin's church and the Rotunda, a historic sculpture of Lord Nelson has been given pride of place. The sculpture had been largely ignored for years because no appropriate location could be found for it. The statue was originally erected by public subscription by

Left. The view of Saint Martin's before improvements – pedestrians are forced under the ring road.

Centre. The new view of Saint Martin's from New Street.

Right. Saint Martin's Church has engaged with its new surroundings, promoting its connections with Future Systems' Selfridges department store and the Rotunda. (Courtesy of St Martin's Centre, design by geothree.co.uk.)

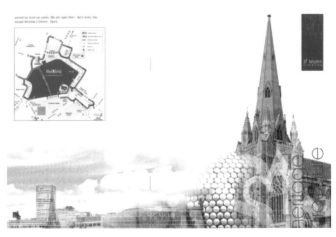

Above. The reinstated statue of Nelson, with the new Selfridges department store in the background.

Top Right. The 1960s Bullring shopping centre, which formed part of the city's post-war reconstruction.

Centre Right. The upper level of the new Bullring square.

Bottom Right. The upper level of the old Bullring space.

Birmingham's citizens in the 19th century, prior to the erection of Nelson's Column in Trafalgar Square. Not only does the statue connect present citizens with the values of the city's past inhabitants, but it also connects them with a major event in the history of their nation.

The landmark of Saint Martin's church has been renovated as part of the new Bullring and two sides of the church are on prime view from its new square. The church has fully engaged with its adventurous new surroundings. It has an 'open door' policy, with community events, historic information, and a popular jazz cafe. It is now regularly teaming with a broad cross section of Birmingham's citizens and visitors. In a sense, the parish church appears to have been elevated to cathedral status.

The Bullring development was realised through a public–private partnership. The three private companies that came together to form the Birmingham Alliance were

Henderson Global Investments and the property companies Hammerson and Land Securities Group. The partners all held land in various parts of the city, but by working in partnership they were able to combine their land, finance, and professional resources with the council's vision and accountability to local citizens.

On the down-side, the 110,000 m^2 (1.2 million sq.ft) of new floor space within the Bullring centre is overwhelmingly for retail use. The lack of mixed use, especially any residential use, and the semi-private nature of the three new shopping malls that surround the new public spaces, have led to criticism that the area will not perform as a proper urban quarter with its own community, and that the striking buildings will soon look out of date. The result could be that the whole area needs to be redeveloped again in thirty years' time – which is hardly sustainable development.

It can, however, also be argued that it is the new public spaces, the physical connectivity, the views, and the public art that have provided the new development with an enduring quality, something that the 1960s Bullring never had. They help to root the new development and give the city of Birmingham a confidence in its identity. The Bullring is now physically connected to the existing retail core and to the series of interconnected public spaces in the western part of the city centre. By connecting with existing high pedestrian flows, new opportunities for growth to spread eastwards have been created.

Independent forecasts have shown that the opening of the Bullring should push Birmingham up to second place in the UK's national ranking of retail destinations, and that the development represents a 40 per cent increase in Birmingham city centre's retail offer. In its first months of opening, over one million people visited the Bullring every week, and visitor numbers are reported to be up in other stores across the eastern part of the city centre. It appears that the new development has helped Birmingham to capture shoppers from neighbouring provincial cities and from London. Only time will tell whether the new retail offer can be sustained without detriment to existing commercial streets within the core area of the city centre.

Developing a truly mixed-use quarter with a variety of uses around new public spaces still appears to be an elusive dream for Birmingham's city centre. This may only be achieved when the city council realises the longer-term community benefits that arise from self-policing mixed-use communities, and when property funding and management companies have to assess whole-life costs of development schemes. The organisational structure, policy, and operational management of both the public and private sector will need to be adapted to accommodate this. Perhaps this could be the next breakthrough for a public–private sector partnership in Birmingham.

Left. Public space at the base of the Rotunda, before improvements.

Right. The same area after improvements.

INFLUENCING THE WIDER REGION

The success of Birmingham's City Centre Design Strategy has drawn many new
visitors to the city. As well as the new residents, shoppers, tourists, and business
people attracted to Birmingham, urban designers, planners, architects, and civic
leaders have also visited to see how change has been planned and delivered. A
new regional development agency, Advantage West Midlands, is now promoting
Birmingham as a model for urban renaissance across the West Midlands region.
New networking opportunities are also being provided, to share experience and
ideas on best practice in urban design and regeneration. Neighbouring local
authorities have been keen to share in the success that has been generated by
Birmingham's improved city centre. Coventry and Walsall provide two examples.

Coventry by Design

Coventry has a population of over 300,000 people and is located less than 25
miles to the south-east of central Birmingham. Although Coventry' origins are
more ancient than those of Birmingham, and it survived as a town of national
architectural and historic importance into the 1930s, it shares a similar industrial
history, much of it focused on car production.

As with Birmingham, Coventry was heavily bombed in the Second World War. It was also subject to post-war redevelopment that destroyed the city's medieval grid pattern to facilitate vehicular accessibility. Coventry was given an inner ring road in the 1960s, which has also served as a concrete collar, segregating various quarters and restricting pedestrian movement. Although 350 buildings dating from before the 17th century survived the war, only 34 remained by 1966.

In January 1999, Coventry City Council commissioned consultants to create their own urban design strategy, Coventry by Design, which was produced by the London-based consultants Urban Initiatives. The urban design strategy shows how a distinctive city centre could be recreated. It defines character areas, where there are surviving homogeneous features, and suggests how they could be developed into distinct quarters, in a similar fashion to Birmingham's City Centre Design Strategy. Coventry by Design shows how pedestrian desire lines and public-transport interchanges could be accommodated, and how breaking the inner ring road could improve pedestrian movement patterns. As with Birmingham's City Centre Design Strategy, its main focus is the creation of a more-legible built environment through the establishment of well-designed public spaces.

The Phoenix Initiative is a city-led partnership that has delivered much of the vision for a better city centre. It has resulted in the creation of new public spaces along a route that connects the cathedral with the transport museum. These are the two dynamic institutions that help to define the special character of Coventry. An improved public realm and a strategic approach to public art are defining features along the Phoenix Trail.

Right. The new public space at the cathedral close – it has been cleared of traffic and is the beginning of a sequence of public spaces that form Coventry's Phoenix Trail.

Far Right. Simple public spaces, cleared of clutter, link Coventry's major visitor attractions.

Far Left. Architecture and art are combined to connect the Phoenix Trail in Coventry with major new public spaces.

Left . The 'Whittle arch' in Coventry flys over a hidden river and leads the eye to the Phoenix Trail. The sculpture has been shortlisted for the prestigious stirling prize.

Walsall's strategy

Walsall is a town that forms part of the West Midlands urban conurbation and is located less than ten miles to the north of Birmingham's city centre. Walsall's design strategy has included linking new and improved public spaces with pedestrianised streets. A major new art gallery has been built within an enhanced quarter based around a canal wharf. An ancient market, which dates back to 1212, has been refurbished, and a dramatic modern bus station set within a new square creates an impressive sense of arrival for those arriving by public transport.

The centrepiece of the strategy is a recently built new town square, located at the heart of the town centre at a major junction that was previously dominated by traffic congestion. The square provides a physical link between all of the major regeneration proposals within their strategy, including the refurbished market, high street, and the new art gallery. A national competition was held for designs for the new square, which was won by the Midlands-based practice Eachus Huckson Landscape Architects.

Public art is a major feature of Walsall's new town square and other regenerated public spaces. The artist Tom Lomax, who produced works of art in Birmingham's Victoria Square, was commissioned to produce new works of art that reflect Walsall's various wealth-generating trades.

Left and below. Walsall's new art gallery. (Courtesy of Walsall MBC.)

Above Centre. Walsall's new public square serves as a focal point to the town centre. (Courtesy of Walsall MBC.)

Above Right. The new public square was initiated as a flagship project to connect all the projects within the broader regeneration strategy.

CONCLUSIONS

The urban design strategies developed for Walsall and Coventry are in part a testimony to the success of Birmingham's City Centre Design Strategy. They show how model projects developed in a regional capital can serve as a beacon for success. Birmingham's strategic approach to urban improvements, and the quality of its new public spaces, has served as a model for other initiatives across the region, which all build up momentum for an urban renaissance. Birmingham is now recognised by the UK Government as being an 'emerging world city' and its urban improvements are being officially championed at 25 designated urban growth centres across the West Midlands region.

A key challenge for Birmingham and other urban areas is how to apply the best practice developed in creating public space in the city centre to the suburban centres and ordinary streets and spaces that make up the modern city.

SUMMARY POINTS

- Birmingham's urban design strategy provided the vision required to strengthen the character of urban quarters, and the land values within them, through creating prestigious new squares that would become major destination points.

- Birmingham's urban design strategy provided the vision for sequences of interconnected squares and pedestrianised streets that would bring people from the centre into the urban quarters, thereby extending the city-centre activity and providing new investment opportunities, not just for office, conference, and entertainment uses, but also for city-centre housing.

- Having strong and enduring support for Birmingham's urban design strategy from a local political leader provided the degree of certainty required for private-sector investors and public-sector decision makers to act in a joined-up way for over a two decade time span

- The improvements to the network of public space within Birmingham's city centre have helped to transform the image and economic performance of the whole city, and have served as a beacon for the regeneration of other urban centres across the West Midlands region.

- It remains to be seen if Birmingham's city centre can attract enough people to sustain the centre and the new quarters, or if pedestrian flows will be sufficient to create lively public spaces in areas such as the far side of the Eastside without accompanying investment in a better public transport network.

- Creation of a mixture of uses (including residential) in the buildings that enclose new public squares has not yet been achieved in Birmingham.

- A challenge remains to apply the best practice gleaned from improving public space in Birmingham's city centre to its suburban centres and to the vast number of streets and spaces that form Europe's largest local authority area.

REFERENCES/FURTHER
READING>

REFERENCES/ FURTHER READING

1   CABE Space (2003).

2   Jacobs, J., *The Death and Life of Great American Cities*, Penguin (1984).

3   Cooper Marcus, C. and Francis, C., *People Places: Design Guidelines for Urban Open Space*, New York, Van Nostrand Reinhold (1993).

4   Whyte, W. H., *The Social Life of Small Urban Spaces*, Conservation Foundation (1980).

5   Moughtin, C., *Urban Design: Street and Square*, Oxford, Butterworth Architecture (1992).

6   Kostof, S., *The City Assembled: The Elements of Urban Form Through History*, London, Thames and Hudson (1999).

7   Gehl, J. and Gemzøe, L., *Public Spaces, Public Life,* Danish Architectural Press (1996).

8   Carmona, M., Heath, T., Oc, T. and Tiesdell, S., *Public Places – Urban Spaces*, Architectural Press (2003).

9   Mumford, L., *The City in History: Its Origins, Its Transformations and Its Prospects*, Harcourt Brace (1961).

10 Zucker, P., *Town and Square*, Columbia University Press (1959).

11 Morris, A. E. J., *History of Urban Form Before the Industrial Revolution*, 3rd edn, Harlow, Longman (1994).

12   Bentley, I., Alcock, A., Murrain, P., McGlynn, S. and Smith, G., *Responsive Environments: A Manual for Designers*, London, Architectural Press (1985).

13   Lynch, K., *The Image of the City*, MIT Press (1976).

14   Alan Baxter Associates for CABE and ODPM, *Paving the Way*, London, Thomas Telford Publishing (2002).

15   Llewelyn-Davies, *The Urban Design Compendium*, for English Partnerships and the Housing Corporation (2000).

16   Sitte, C., *The Art of Building Cities*, Reinhold Publishing Corporation (1945) (originally published 1889, now out of print).

17   Atkinson, R., 'Discourses of Partnership and Empowerment in Contemporary British Urban Regeneration', *Urban Studies*, Vol. 36, No. 1, 1999, pp. 107–19.

18   Ward, S.V., Public–private partnerships, in Cullingworth, B.(ed.), *British Planning, 50 Years of Urban and Regional Policy*, Athlone Press, London (1999).

19   Ministry of Housing and Local Government and Ministry of Transport, *Town centres: approach to renewal, Planning Bulletin No 1*. London, HMSO (1962).

20   Ministry of Housing and Local Government and Ministry of Transport, *Town centres: cost and control of redevelopment, Planning Bulletin No. 3*, London, HMSO (1963).

21   CABE/DETR, *By Design: Urban Design in the Planning System: Towards Better Practice*. London, Thomas Telford Publishing (2000).

22   Lieberman, E., *People's needs and preferences as the basis of San Francisco's downtown open space plan*. Paper presented at the 8th conference of the International Association for the Study of People and Their Physical Surroundings, Berlin, July 1984.

23   Andrews, J. H., 'The TIFs Go On', *Planning* (APA), Vol. 65, No. 1, January 1999.

24   Zeisel, J., *Inquiry by Design: Tools for Environment – Behaviour Research*, Cambridge, Cambridge University Press (1984).

25   *Fleet 2000*, produced by the Joint Centre for Urban Design, Oxford Brookes University, unpublished (1996).

26   Project for Public Places Inc., *Chase Manhattan Plaza Study*, 1975, mimeo (1984), p. 28.

27   Oxford Institute of Retail Management, *The Health of the High Street*, OXIRM Research Paper, OXIRM, Oxford (1986).

28   URBED, *Vital and Viable Town Centres; Meeting the Challenge*, London, HMSO (1994).

29   Kostof, S., *The City Shaped: Urban Patterns and Meaning Through History*, London, Thames and Hudson (1991).

30   Hillier, B. and Hanson, J., *The Social Logic of Space*, Cambridge, Cambridge University Press. (1984).

31 Hillier, B. and Hanson, J., *The Architects' Journal*, 30 November 1983 pp. 43–60.

32 *The Architect's Journal*, 15 April 1992 pp. 42–43.

33 *Building Design*, 2 May, 1997 pp. 14–15.

34 Hillier B., speaking at Kensington Town Hall, London, 24 March 1998.

35 Bacon, E. N., *Design of Cities*, revised edition, London, Thames and Hudson (1975).

36 *Streetscape*, Royal Borough of Kensington and Chelsea, London (2004).

37 Lewis, C. S., *Surprised by Joy: The Shape of My Early Life*, London, G. Bles (1955).

38 Hass-Klau, C., 'Where and Why People Walk', *Third Annual Quality Streetscapes Conference*, Landor Publishing (1998).

39 Apel, D. and Pharoah, T. M., *Transport Concepts in European Cities*, Aldershot, Avebury (1995).

40 Organization for Economic Cooperation and Development, *Streets for People*, Paris, OECD (1974).

41 J. Worthington, Transport Nodes 2000+, *Planning in London*, April 2000, pp. 19–21.

42 Cullen, G., *The Concise Townscape*, London, Architectural Press (1971).

43 L'Enfant's Washington, *National Geographic*, Vol. 180, No. 2., August 1991.

44 Goldsteen, J. B. and Elliot, C. D., *Designing America: Creating Urban Identity*, New York, Von Nostrand Reinhold (1994).

45 George A. R., Babylon revisited: archaeology and philology in harness, *Antiquity*, Vol. 67, 1993, p. 737.

46 Sitte, C., City Planning According to Artistic Principles (1889); translation in: Collins, G. R., *Camillo Sitte: The Birth of Modern City Planning*, New York, Rizzoli (1986).

47 Pushkarev, B., and Zuplan, J. M., *Urban Space for People*, London, MIT Press (1975), p. 165.

48 Lynch, K., *A Theory of Good City Form*, MIT Press (1981).

49 Carr, S., Francis, M., Rivlin, L. and Stone, A., *Public Space*, Cambridge, Cambridge University Press (1992).

50 Gehl, J., Mennisker til Fods, *Arkitekten*, Vol. 70 (2) (1968), pp. 429–446.

51 Krier, R., *Urban Space*, London, Academy Editions (1979).

52 Alberti, c. 1442, quoted from the 1755 Edition: Alberti, L. B., *On the Art of Building in 10 Books*, London, MIT Press (1988).

53 Bomford, D. and Finaldi, G., *Venice Through Canaletto's Eyes*, London, National Gallery Publications (1998).

54   Gideon, S., *Space, Time and Architechture: the growth of a new tradition*, Cambridge (MA), Harvard University Press (1942).

55   Baulch, J., *Towards Good Mixed Use Districts*, unpublished MA dissertation, JCUD, Oxford Brookes University (1993).

56   Olgyay, V., *Design With Climate: Bioclimatic Approach to Architectural Regionalism*, New York, Van Nostrand Reinhold (1992).

57   Terence O'Rourke plc, *Planning for Passive Solar Design*, Garston, BRECSU/BRE (1999).

58   Gehl, J., *Life Between Buildings*, New York, Van Nostrand Reinhold (1987).

59   Pushkarev, B. and Zupan, J. M., *Urban Space For Pedestrians: A Report of the Regional Plan Association*, MIT Press (1975).

60   Lynch, K. and Hack, G., *Site Planning*, MIT Press (1984).

61   Arnold, H. F., *Trees in Urban Design*, Van Nostrand Reinhold (1993).

62   Whyte, W., *The Social Life of Small Urban Spaces*, Conservation Foundation (1980).

63   Altman, I., *The Environment and Social Behaviour: privacy, personal space, territory crowding*, Monterey (CA), Brooks/Lok Publishing Co. (1975).

64   Dornbusch, D. M. and Gelb, P., High rise impacts on the use of parks and plazas, in Conway, D. J. (ed.), *Human Response to Tall Buildings*, Stroudsberg, Dowden, Hutchinson and Ross (1979).

65   Bourgeois, J.-L., *Spectacular Vernacular: A New Appreciation of Desert Architecture*, Salt Lake City, Peregrino Smith Books, p. 87–9 (1983).

66   Oliver, P. (ed.), *Shelter, Sign and Symbol*, London, Barrie and Jenkins (1975).

67   Joardar, S. D. and Neill, J. W., The subtle differences in configurations of small public spaces. *Landscape Architecture*, Vol. 68 (11) (1978), pp. 487–491.

68   Institution of Lighting Engineers (1997).

69   Hunt, T., *Building Jerusalem: The Rise and Fall of the Victorian City*, London, Weidenfeld & Nicolson (2004).

70   Tibbalds, Colbourne, Karski, Williams (for Birmingham City Council), *City Centre Design Strategy* (1990).

71   Advantage West Midlands (2000).

72   Urban Task Force, *Urban Renaissance: Sharing the Vision*, London, DETR (1999).

FURTHER READING

Adams, D., 'Buying Made Easy', *Planning Issue* 1323 (1999).

Alexander, C., *A New Theory of Urban Design*, Oxford University Press (1987).

Aldous, T., *Urban Villages: A Concept for Creating Mixed-Use Urban Developments on a Sustainable Scale*, Urban Villages Group (1992).

Altman, I. and Zube, E. H., *Public Places and Spaces*, Plenum (1989).

Beer, A., *Environmental Planning for Site Development*, London, Spon (1991).

Berridge, J., *Yonge Dundas Redevelopment Project*, Ontario Municipal Board City of Toronto (1998).

Birmingham City Council, *Convention Centre Quarter: Planning and Urban Design Framework* (1990).

Birmingham City Council, *The Bull Ring Area, The Next Step* (1994).

Broadbent, G., *Emerging Concepts in Urban Design*, Van Nostrand Reinhold (1990).

Castells, M., *The Information City*, Blackwell (1989).

Cohen, B., *The Cultural Science of Man: The Origins of Civilization*, London, volume 2, Codek (1988).

Fraser, W. D., *Principles of Property Investment and Pricing*, Macmillan (1984).

Girouard, M., *Cities and People*, Yale University Press (1985).

Harris, C. M., *Illustrated Dictionary of Historic Architecture*, Constable and Co. (1977).

Hass-Klau, C., *The Pedestrian and City Traffic*, London, Belhaven Press (1990).

Hayward, R. and McGlynn, S., *Making Better Places: Urban Design Now*, Butterworth Heinemann (1993).

JCUD, *Principles of Successful Main Streets*, unpublished issues project, Oxford Brooks University, March (1995).

Korosec-Serfaty, P., *The Main Square*, Aris (1978).

McHarg, I., *Design with Nature*, Natural History Press (1969).

Robins, K. and Hepworth, M., 'Electronic Spaces: New Technologies and the Future of Cities', *Futures*, April 1988.

Robinson, F. and Shaw, K., 'What Works in Those Inner Cities?', *Town and Country Planning*, Vol. 66., No. 6, 1997.

Schumacher, E. F., *A Guide for the Perplexed*, Penguin (1977).

Specter D. K., *Urban Spaces*, Greenwich, New York Graphic Society (1974)

Tollit, M., *The Search for a Public Realm,* unpublished MA dissertation, JCUD, Oxford Brookes University (1994).

Trancik, R., *Finding Lost Space*, Van Nostrand Reinhold (1986).

Urban Initiatives, *Coventry Urban Design Study*, Coventry City Council (1999).

Ward, S., 'Public-Private Partnerships', in: Cullingworth (ed.), *British Planning*, London, Athlone Press (1999).

Webb, M., *The City Square*, Thames and Hudson (1993).

Wycherley, R. E., *How the Greek's Built Citites*, Macmillan (1962).

APPENDIX I>

APPENDIX I
URBAN DESIGN TERMINOLOGY

The following descriptions are loosely based on the categories developed by Kevin Lynch in *The Image of the City* (1976).

Paths: The network of channels along which people within the city move, such as footpaths, streets, canals, cycle paths, etc. They are like blood vessels that bring the lifeblood – people – to all parts of the city.

Nodes: These are the most accessible sites within the city, located at the intersection of pathways, where there tends to be a greater concentration of people. The node is a focal point, a space that a person has a sense of entering into, and as such it provides a sense of interest and incident along the pathways that connect with it. There will often be a hierarchy of nodes and public squares within a city, with the main city square being the most accessible node.

Landmarks: Points of reference that support way-finding and orientation when travelling through the city. Landmarks provide perspective within the townscape, and can provide visually satisfying emphasis to a long view or focal point. They are often located within public squares or on the buildings around a square, where they mark its presence from the surrounding area. They are often of historic and cultural significance. An example would be an obelisk within a city square that can be seen from far down approaching streets.

Views and vistas: Open sight lines through the city that are worthy of preservation because they reveal built or natural forms that are of special significance to the city. The frame and backdrop to a view is also likely to be important.

Edges: Linear elements that form boundaries or barriers to different parts of the city. Edges are either not used as paths or are seen from positions where their path nature is obscured, such as a railway line or urban motorway. They are obstacles that have to be bridged if the areas they separate are to be connected.

Districts: Distinct and largely intact geographical 'quarters' of the city that have homogenous qualities. These qualities provide the district with its unique identity. They may relate to the layout of streets and public spaces, to prevailing uses, to architectural styles, or to the people that live or work there.

APPENDIX II>

APPENDIX II
THE STATUE
OF CHARLES I

The statue of King Charles I that now stands in Trafalgar Square has had an interesting history. When King Charles I was forced to leave London as a result of Oliver Cromwell's defence of Parliament, the statue of him was apparently taken into hiding at Hammersmith in west London. It was hidden by Royalists, who feared that Cromwell would have it smelted down. When the monarchy was eventually reinstated the statue was placed in its current location. Eleanor's Cross had previously stood upon the same spot. This was one of several crosses erected in the 13th century to mark where the queen's coffin rested on its route back to London for burial. A reconstruction of the cross now stands in front of Charing Cross railway station.

INDEX>

INDEX

Note: page numbers in italics refer to illustrations.

ENDNOTE>

The Lord will guide you always;
he will satisfy your needs in a sun-scorched land
and will strengthen your frame.
You will be like a well-watered garden,
like a spring whose waters never fail.
Your people will rebuild the ancient ruins
and will raise up the age-old foundations;
you will be called Repairer of Broken Walls,
Restorer of Streets with Dwellings
Isaiah 58 v11–1